Social Media Marketing

A Practitioner Guide

Fourth Edition

Copyright © 2017-20 Svend Hollensen, Philip Kotler and
Marc Oliver Opresnik

All rights included.

Texts:	© Copyright by Svend Hollensen, Philip Kotler and Marc Oliver Opresnik
Cover:	Malte Mumbeck / Tabea Heinrich
Publisher:	Opresnik Management Consulting
Series:	Opresnik Management Guides, Book 14
Print:	Amazon Fulfillment, an Amazon company

ISBN-13	9798643250623

Bibliografische Information der Deutschen Nationalbibliothek

Die Deutsche Nationalbibliothek verzeichnet diese Publikation in der Deutschen Nationalbibliografie; detaillierte bibliografische Daten sind im Internet über http://dnb.d-nb.de abrufbar

Social Media Marketing

A Practitioner Guide

Fourth Edition

by

Prof. Svend Hollensen, Ph.D., University of Southern Denmark,

Prof. Philip Kotler, Ph.D., Kellogg School of Management, Northwestern University, USA,

and

Prof. Marc Oliver Opresnik, Ph.D., Technische Hochschule Lübeck, Germany

To Jonna, Nanna and Julie

Svend Hollensen

To my wife Nancy, my lifelong companion and muse.

Philip Kotler

To Charlie, Christine and Simon

Marc Oliver Opresnik

Preface to the Fourth Edition

'The world is flat' is the title of a book written by Pulitzer prize winner Thomas L. Friedman in 2005. According to him, the beginning of the twenty-first century will be remembered not for military conflicts or political events, but for a whole new age of globalization – a 'flattening' of the world.

Friedman was right: The rapid explosion of advanced technologies now means that all out of a sudden knowledge pools and resources have connected all over the planet, levelling the playing field as never before, so that each business and entrepreneur is potentially a customer and at the same time an equal competitor of the other. The rules of the game have changed forever –and these do account for all business sectors and functions alike. Companies, organizations and entrepreneurs all have to run faster in order to stay in the same place.

Against this background, marketing communication is also undergoing rapid development as the way of communicating has changed forever. The increasing popularity of blogging, podcasting, and social networks enable the modern world customers to broadcast their views about a product or service to a potential audience of billions, and the proliferation of Internet access to even the poorest communities gives everyone who wants to the tools to address issues with products and companies. Consequently, advertising does not work anymore, at least not like it used to do in the past. In former times, marketers used to be able to buy some advertising time on TV or a paper ad, but nowadays more and more customers are using Video on Demand (VoD)and get their news online. The conversations that took place under industrial broadcast media about companies' products happened in rather small groups, and their influence and impact disappeared as soon as they were spoken. Nowadays, the conversations happen in real time and in front of potentially billions of people, and they are archived for decades to come.

Of course, there are ample opportunities as well: Small companies do not have to outspend the biggest companies anymore; now they can outsmart them with sophisticated social media marketing strategies. They do not have to spend thousands on focus groups or marketing research projects as they potentially have their market's pulse at their fingertips with online searches.

This completely updated and extended fourth edition of 'Social Media Marketing' guides through the maze of communities, platforms, and social media tools so that markers can decide which ones to use, and how to use them most effectively. With an objective approach and clear, straightforward language, it shows how to plan and implement campaigns intelligently, and then measure results and track return on investment. For beginners overwhelmed by too many choices as well as seasoned professionals eager to improve their game, this comprehensive book is full of tactics that have been proven to work in the real marketing world. This book will take you beyond the jargon to social media marketing mastery. But that is not all. This book is like a guide through your social media marketing strategy process. All the insights will naturally be explained, but you will also learn how to arrive at them. So here you will read, for example, not only that you need to communicate you brand in a consistent way to enhance exposure, but you also need to learn how to set up your communication strategy as a good basis for increasing and maintain your value add and brand proposition – all written in a concise and easy to understand manner.

This book will thus be a real guide. Apply yourself to the appropriate concepts and practical advice contained within it! Train your skills! When the Irish-British playwright and Nobel laureate George Bernard Shaw was asked how he had learned to be so compelling and engaging a speaker, he replied: 'I've learned it the same way I learned to skate - with perseverance I made a fool of myself until I could do it.' By intensive reading and working with this book and by applying the tools it contains for successful social media marketing communication in your daily life, you will become a social media marketing professional!

In the development of this text several reviewers have been involved, whom we would like to thank for their important and valuable contribution. Especially, we would like to thank Professor Marko Sarstedt, Chair of Marketing at Otto-von-Guericke-Universität Magdeburg, Germany, University of Southern Denmark and the Technische Hochschule Lübeck.

Throughout the writing period there has only been one constant in our lives – our families. Without them, nothing would have been possible. Thus, Professor Svend Hollensen, Professor Philip Kotler and Professor Marc Oliver Opresnik dedicate this book to their families.

Svend Hollensen, Philip Kotler and Marc Oliver Opresnik

May 2021

Contents

1. Social Media Marketing Planning

1.1 Introduction to Marketing Planning

Marketing is the organization function charged with defining customer targets and the best way to satisfy their needs and wants competitively and profitably. Because consumers and business buyers face an abundance of suppliers seeking to satisfy their every need, companies and not-for-profit organizations cannot survive today by simply doing a good job. They must do an excellent job if they are to remain in the increasingly competitive global marketplace. Many studies have demonstrated that the key to profitable performance is knowing and satisfying target customers with competitively superior offers. This process takes place today in an increasingly global, technical, and competitive environment.

There are some key reasons why marketing planning has become so important.

Recent years have witnessed an intensifying of competition in many markets. Many factors have contributed to this, but amongst some of the more significant are the following:

- A growth of global competition, as barriers to trade have been lowered and global communications improved significantly.
- the role of the multinational conglomerate has increased. This ignores geographical and other boundaries and looks for profit opportunities on a global scale.
- In some economies, legislation and political ideologies have aimed at fostering entrepreneurial and 'free market' values.
- Continual technological innovation, giving rise to new sources of competition for established products, services and markets.

The importance of competition and competitor analysis in contemporary strategic marketing cannot be overemphasized. Indeed, because of this we shall be looking at this aspect in more depth in later chapters. This importance is now widely accepted amongst both marketing academics and practitioners. Successful marketing in a competitive economy is about competitive success and that in addition to a customer focus a true marketing orientation also combines competitive positioning.

The marketing concept holds that the key to achieving organizational goals lies in determining the needs and wants of target markets, and delivering the desired 'satisfaction' more effectively and resourcefully than competitors (Hollensen, 2006).

Marketing planning is an approach adopted by many successful, market-focused companies. While it is by no means a new tool, the degree of objectivity and thoroughness with which it is applied varies significantly.

Marketing planning can be defined as the structured process of researching and analyzing the marketing situations, developing and documenting marketing objectives, strategies, and programs, and implementing, evaluating, and controlling activities to achieve the goals. This systematic process of marketing planning involves analyzing the environment and the company's capabilities, and deciding on courses of action and ways to implement those decisions. As the marketing environment is so changeable that paths to new opportunities can open in an instant, even as others become obscured or completely blocked, marketing planning must be approached as an adaptable, ongoing process rather than a rigid, static annual event.

The outcome of this structured process is the marketing plan, a document that summarizes what the marketer has learned about the marketplace and outlines how the firm plans to reach its marketing objectives. In addition, the marketing plan not only documents the organization's marketing strategies and displays the activities that employees will implement to reach the marketing objectives, but it entails the mechanisms that will measure progress toward the objectives and allows for adjustments if actual results take the organization off course.

Marketing plans generally cover a 1-year-period, although some may project activities and financial performance further into the future. Marketers must start the marketing planning process at least several months before the marketing plan is scheduled to go into operation; this allows sufficient time for thorough research and analysis, management review and revision, and coordination of resources among functions and business units.

Marketing planning inevitably involves change. It is a process that includes deciding currently what to do in the future with a full appreciation of the resource position; the need to set clear, communicable, measurable objectives; the development of alternative courses of action; and a means of assessing the best route towards the achievement of specified objectives. Marketing planning is designed to assist the process of marketing decision making under prevailing conditions of risk and uncertainty (Hollensen and Opresnik, 2015).

Above all the process of marketing planning has several benefits (Hollensen, 2006):

- **Consistency**: The individual marketing action plans must be consistent with the overall corporate plan and with the other departmental or functional plans.
- **Responsibility**: Those who have responsibility for implementing the individual parts of the marketing plan will know what their responsibilities are and can have their performance assessed against these plans. Marketing planning requires management staff to make clear judgmental statements about assumptions, and it enables a control system to be designed and established whereby performance can be assessed against pre-defined criteria.
- **Communication**: Those implementing the plans will also know that the overall objectives are and how they personally may contribute in this respect.
- **Commitment**: If the plans are agreed upon by those involved in their implementation, as well as by those who will provide the resources, the plans do stimulate a group commitment to their implementation, and ultimately lead to better strategy-implementation.

Plans must be specific to the organization and its current situation. There is not one system of planning but many systems, and a planning process must be tailor-made for a particular firm in a specific set of conditions. Marketing planning as a functional activity has to be set in a corporate planning framework. There is an underlying obligation for any organization adopting marketing planning systems to set a clearly defined business mission as the basis from which the organizational direction can develop. Without marketing planning, it is more difficult to guide research and development (R&D) and new product development (NPD); set required standards for suppliers; guide the sales force in terms of what to emphasize, set realistic, achievable targets, avoid competitor actions or changes in the marketplace. Above all, businesses which fail to incorporate marketing planning into their marketing activities may therefore not be able to develop a sustainable competitive advantage in their markets (Hollensen, 2006).

1.2 The Main Stages in Developing a Digital Marketing Plan

A social media marketing plan is the summary of everything the company plan to do in social media marketing and hope to achieve for the business using social networks. This plan should comprise an audit of where the customers are today, goals for where you want them to be soon, and all the social media tools that the company wants to use to get there.

In general, the more specific the company can get with their plan, the more effective they will be in the plan's implementation. It is important to keep it concise. The plan will guide the company's actions, but it will also be a measure by which to determine whether the company is succeeding or failing. Figure 1.1 illustrates the several stages that should be gone through to arrive at a digital marketing plan (Gilmore et al., 2001; Day, 2002).

Step 1: Create social media marketing objectives

The first step to any social media marketing strategy is to establish the objectives and goals that the company hope to achieve. Having these objectives also allows the company to quickly react when social marketing media campaigns are not meeting the company's expectations. Without objectives, the company has no means of evaluating success or proving their social media **Return on Investment (ROI)**. These goals should be aligned with the broader marketing strategy, so that the social media efforts drive toward the business objectives. If the social media marketing plan is shown to support the overall business objective, the company is more likely to get executive

4

and employee buy-in and investment. The company should try to go beyond popular metrics such as Retweets and Likes. Focus should be more on advanced metrics such as ,number of leads generated', web referrals, and conversion rate. The company should also use the SMART framework when setting their objectives:

- **Specific** – target a specific area for improvement.
- **Measurable** – quantify or at least suggest an indicator of progress.
- **Achievable** – Agreed and aligned with corporate goals.
- **Realistic** – state what results can realistically be achieved, given available resources.
- **Time-related** – specify when the result(s) can be achieved.

Figure 1.1: The stages of building a digital marketing plan

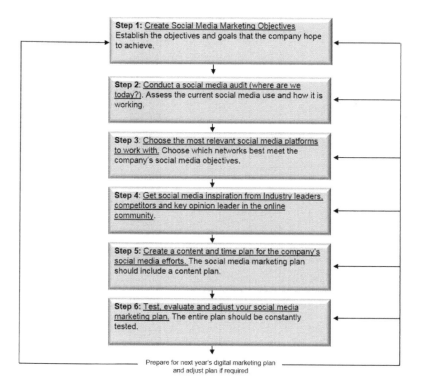

Example: *'In Social Publishing we will share photos that communicate our company culture. We will do this by posting a total of ten photos a week on any of the photo sharing social media sites. The target for each week is at least in total 100 likes and 30 comments.'*

A simple way to start the social media marketing plan is by writing down at least three social media objectives.

Step 2: Conduct a social media audit (where are we today?)

Prior to creating your social media marketing plan, the company needs to assess their current social media use and how it is working. This means figuring out who is currently connecting with the company and its brand via social media, which social media sites the company target market uses, and how the social media presence compares to the competitors. For this purpose, the following social media audit template can be used:

Table 1.1: Social Media Audit template (current situation)

Presence on Social media platform	URL	Internal respon- sible for main- taining social media	Social media mission	Current number of followers	Main competitor's number of followers
etc.					

Once the audit is conducted the company should have a clear picture of every social media platform representing the business, who runs or controls them, and what purpose they serve. This audit should be maintained regularly, especially as the company scale up their business.

It should also be evident which social media platforms (accounts) need to be updated and which need to be deleted altogether. If the audit uncovers for example a fake branded Twitter profile, it should be reported. Reporting fake accounts will help ensure that people searching for the company online only connect with the accounts that are managed by the company itself.

As part of the social media audit the company may also want to create mission statements for each social media platform (network). These one-sentence declarations will help to focus on a very specific objective for Instagram, Facebook, or any other social media network. They will guide the actions and help guiding back on track if the efforts begin to lag.

Example of Mission statement for a presence on the Snapchat platform: *'We will use Snapchat to share the CSR side of our company and connect with younger prospect customers among 15-40 years old.'*

The company should be able to determine the purpose of every social media platform it has, for example Snapchat. If it cannot determine the mission for each social media platform, the platform & profile should probably be deleted.

Before it is possible to determine which social media platforms are right for the business, the company should find out who the audience is for each platform and what they want. The company should know which tools to use to gather demographic and behavioral data, and how to target the customers it wants.

Step 3: Choose the most relevant social media platforms to work with

Once you've finished with your social media audit, it is time to choose the online presence. Choose which networks best meet the company's social media missions and objectives. If there is not already a social media profile on each network/platform the company focuses on, it should build them from the ground up with the broader mission and audience in mind. Each social network has a unique audience and should be treated differently. If the company has some existing platforms, it is time to update and refine them to get the best possible results.

Optimizing profiles for SEO (Search Engine Optimization) can help to generate more web traffic to the company's online social media platforms. Cross-promoting social platforms can extend the reach of content. In general, social media profiles should be filled out completely, and images and text should be optimized for the social network in question.

Step 4: Get social media inspiration from Industry leaders, competitors and key opinion leader in the online community

If the company is not sure what kinds of content and information will get the most engagement, then the company, for inspiration, can look to what others in the industry are sharing. The company can also use social media listening to see how it can distinguish itself from competitors and appeal to an audience it might be missing.

Opinion leaders among consumers ('Influencers') can also offer social media inspiration, not only through the content that they share but in the way that they phrase their messages. The company can try and see how its target audience writes Tweets, and it could strive to write in a similar style. It can also learn their habits - when they share and why - and use that as a basis for the social media marketing plan.

A final source of social media inspiration is industry leaders. There are giants who do an incredible job of social media marketing, from Red Bull and Taco Bell to Turkish Airlines. Companies in every industry imaginable have managed to distinguish themselves through advanced social media strategies.

The company can follow industry leaders and see if they have shared any social media advice or insight elsewhere on the web.

Step 5: Create a content and time plan for the company's social media efforts

The social media marketing plan should include a content marketing plan, comprised of strategies for content creation, as well as an editorial calendar (time plan) for when the content should be shown online. Having great content to share and the right timing will be essential to succeeding at social media marketing.

The content marketing plan should answer the following questions:

- What types of content the company intends to post and promote on social media?
- Who will create the content?
- How often will the company post content?
- What is the target audience for each type of content?
- How you the company promote the content?

The editorial calendar lists the dates and times the company intends to publish blogs, Instagram and Facebook posts, Tweets, and other content that is planned to use during the social media campaigns.

The company can create the calendar and then schedule their messaging in advance rather than updating constantly throughout the day. This gives it the opportunity to work hard on the language and format of these messages rather than writing them on the fly whenever company employees have time. The company should make sure that the content reflects the mission statement that are assigned to each social media profile/platform. If the purpose of the LinkedIn account is to generate leads, the company should make sure that it is sharing enough lead generation content. The company can establish a content matrix that defines what share of the social media platform is allocated to different types of posts. For example:

- 30 percent of content will try to get new potential visitors to actually visit the company's social media platform.
- 30 percent of content will support enterprise profit objectives in general (lead generation, selling, cross-selling, etc.)
- 20 percent of content will try drive back visitors to your blog (content supporting loyal visitors)
- 20 percent of content will be about the company's HR, CSR and culture

If the company is unsure of how to allocate their resources, a safe bet is to follow this rule:

- One-third of the company's social content promotes its business, converts visitors, and generates profit
- One-third of the social content should share ideas and stories from thought leaders in the industry or similar businesses
- One-third of the social content should be personal interactions with your audience (e.g. blogging)

Step 6: Test, evaluate and adjust your social media marketing plan

To find out what adjustments need to be made to your social media marketing strategy, you should constantly be testing. Build testing capabilities into every action you take on social networks. For example, you could track the number of clicks your links get on a particular platform using URL shorteners. Furthermore, it is possible to measure track page visits driven by social media with Google Analytics.

Record and analyze your successes and failures, and then adjust your social media marketing plan in response.

Surveys are also a great way to gauge success - online and offline. The company can ask their social media followers, email list, and website visitors how they are doing on social media. This direct approach is often very effective. Then ask your offline customers if social media had a role in their purchasing. This insight might prove invaluable when you look for areas to improve. In Section 5.1 it is possible to learn more about the use of different Social Media metrics, for example how to measure social media ROI for the business.

The most important thing to understand about the social media marketing plan is that it should be constantly changing. As new networks emerge, the company may want to add them to their plan. As the company is attaining missions and objectives for each social media platform, it will need to set new targets. Unexpected challenges will arise that is needed to address. As the company is scaling up its business, it might need to add new roles or grow the social presence for different products or regions.

The company should rewrite its social media marketing plan to reflect its latest insights, and make sure that the team is aware of what has been updated.

2. Digital Marketing Research

2.1 Introduction to Marketing Research

The term market research refers to gathering, analyzing and presenting information that is related to a well-defined problem. Hence the focus of market research is a specific problem or project with a beginning and an end.

Market research differs from a decision support system (DSS), which is information gathered and analyzed on a continual basis. In practice, market research and DSS are often hard to differentiate, so they will be used interchangeably in this context.

Marketers have the idea that different customers should be treated differently to maximize the relationship with the best ones and minimize the involvement with the worst ones. Information technology helps to realize that desire. The reality comes at a cost, however, as relationship marketing presents a new set of challenges both to marketers and information systems managers. To succeed, an effective cross-functional team of information systems and marketing specialists must work harmoniously. In the past, the two groups barely understood or tolerated each other. On a positive note, a new breed of cross-disciplinary executives exists. They understand both marketing and technology. Overall, the most successful implementation will require true collaboration (Crie Micheaux, 2006; Hollensen and Opresnik, 2015).

To be useful to organizations, knowledge tools must be accessible to mainstream users. They must be understandable and useful to marketing managers, not just statistical experts and information systems managers. To overcome potential problems in applicability, marketers must insist that several key goals be achieved. They include:

- **putting the problem in the marketer's terms,** including viewing the data from a marketing model perspective. Often the job of knowledge discovery is performed by analysts whose primary training is in statistics and data analysis. It is likely that these analysts do not have the same perspective as marketers. To be useful to marketing, the findings must be in a form that marketers can understand;

- **presenting results in a manner that is useful for the business problem at hand.** The foremost benefit of the analysis and the job of the analyst is to help solve business problems and increase or diminish the value of the analysis;

- **providing support for specific key business analyses,** marketers need to know about segmentation, market response, segment reachability. Knowledge discovery tools must support these analyses from the beginning;

- **providing support for an extensive and iterative exploratory process.** Realistic knowledge discovery is not simple and not linear. It is an interactive and iterative learning process. Initial results are fed back into the process to increase accuracy. The process takes time and can have a long lifespan.

2.2 Online (Internet) Research Methods

The Internet is no longer confined to the boundaries of the personal computer screen but has become a medium for the masses. Many researchers are amazed at how efficiently surveys can be conducted, tabulated and analyzed on the Web. Additionally, online data collection lets marketers use complex study designs once considered either too expensive or too cumbersome to execute via traditional means. While initial forays were fraught with technical difficulties and methodological hurdles recent developments have begun to expose the medium's immense potential.

The earliest online tools offered little more than the ability to deploy paper-based questionnaires to Internet users. Today, however, online tools and services are available with a wide range of features at a wide range of prices.

For the international market researcher, the major advantages and disadvantages of online surveys are the following (Grossnickle and Raskin, 2001).

Advantages of online surveys

- **Low financial resource implications:** the scale of the online survey is not associated with finance, i.e. large-scale surveys do not require greater financial resources than small surveys. Expenses related to self-administered postal surveys are usually in the form of outward and return postage, photocopying, etc., none of which is associated with online surveys.
- **Short response time:** online surveys allow questionnaires to be delivered instantly to their recipients, irrespective of their geographical location. Fast survey execution allows for most interviews to be completed within a week or so.
- **Saving time with data collection and analysis:** the respective questionnaire can be programmed so that responses can feed automatically into the data analysis software (SPSS, SAS, Excel, etc.), thus saving time and resources associated with the data entry process. Furthermore, this avoids associated data transcription errors.
- **Visual stimuli:** this can be evaluated, unlike CATI.

Disadvantages of online surveys

- **Respondents have no physical addresses:** the major advantage of postal over online surveys is that respondents have physical addresses, whereas not everyone has an electronic address. This is an international marketing research problem in geographical areas where the penetration of the Internet is not as high as in Europe and North America. For cross-country surveys the multimode approach (i.e. a combination of online and postal survey) compensates for the misrepresentation of the general population.
- **Guarding respondents' anonymity:** traditional mail surveys have advantages in guarding respondents' anonymity. Sensitive issues, which may prevent respondents from giving sincere answers, should be addressed via the post rather than online.
- **Time necessary to download pages:** problems may arise with older browsers that fail to display HTML questionnaires properly,

and also with the appearance of the questionnaires in different browsers (Internet Explorer, Netscape).

Response rates to e-mail questionnaires vary according to the study context. Various factors have been found to inhibit response to e-mail or Internet data collection. These factors include poor design of e-mail questionnaires, lack of anonymity and completion incentives. By addressing these factors in the context of specific research objectives it may provide a way to tackle non-response to e-mail questionnaires. Incentives should be used to encourage response rates, especially if the e-mail questionnaires are lengthy. Potential respondents are likely to trade off their anonymity if incentives are used. The researcher can easily negotiate completion incentives if the sampling frame derives from a company's database (Michaelidou and Dibb, 2006).

Online Quantitative Market Research (E-mail and Web-based Surveys)

Online surveys can be conducted through e-mail or they can be posted on the Web and the URL provided (a password is optional depending on the nature of the research) to the respondents who have already been approached. When a wide audience is targeted the survey can be designed as a pop-up survey, which would appear as a Web-based questionnaire in a browser window while users are browsing the respective websites. Such a Web-based survey is appropriate for a wide audience, where all the visitors to certain websites have an equal chance to enter the survey.

However, the researcher's control over respondents entering the Web-based surveys is lower than for e-mail surveys. One advantage of Web-based surveys is the better display of the questionnaire, whereas e-mail software still suffers from certain limitations in terms of design tools and offering interactive and clear presentation. However, these two modes of survey may be mixed, combining the advantages of each (Ilieva et al., 2002).

Online Qualitative Market Research

There are many interesting opportunities to conduct international qualitative market research quickly and at relatively low cost, without too much travelling involved (Hollensen and Opresnik, 2015):

- **Saving money on travelling costs, etc.:** many qualitative researchers often have to travel to countries in which research is conducted, briefing local moderators and viewing some groups or holding interviews to get a grasp of the local habits and attitudes. This leads to high travelling costs and increases the time needed to execute the fieldwork. It usually takes one or two weeks to recruit the respondents, and one or two weeks before the analysis can start. In online research the respondents can be recruited and interviewed from any computer anywhere in the world. Nearly everyone who is connected to the Internet knows how to use chat rooms. Fieldwork may start two days after briefing, and the analysis may start straight after the last interview based on complete and accurate transcripts, with each comment linked to the respective respondent.

- **Cross-country qualitative research:** international online research is particularly interesting for multinational companies that sell their products on a global scale and are afraid to build the global marketing strategy on research which has been conducted in only a few of these countries. Online qualitative research could serve as an additional multi-country check. This is not intended to give insight into the psychology of customers but rather to check whether other countries or cultures may add to the general picture, which has been made on the basis of qualitative face-to-face research.

One of the limitations with, for example, online focus groups is that they seem to generate less interaction between members than the face-to-face groups. Discussions between respondents occur, but they are less clear and coherent.

2.3 Marketing Research Based on Web 2.0

Today, maybe 80 percent of international marketers' need for international marketing data are addressed by conducting a market-research project.

In future, the leading edge MNEs —probably led by consumer packaged goods and technologically driven companies —will look for answers to 80 percent of their marketing issues by 'catching' already available data.

Some of the data sources and tools available through the Web 2.0 will include the following (Hollensen and Opresnik, 2015):

- **Mobile Data:** One of the biggest opportunities for marketers is the opportunity to collect real-time geographic information about consumers and to geo-target consumers. GPS-enabled smart phones penetrating worldwide markets at an exponential rate coupled with an ongoing increase in cellular bandwidth and data processing speed will result in the opportunity to target the right consumer not only at the right time but at the right place. Major information firms such as Google and innovative start-ups are leading the way in utilizing such readily available data sources in real time.

- **User-generated Content and Text Mining:** Web 2.0 provides gathering places for Internet users in social-network sites (e.g. Facebook, Twitter), blogs, forums, and chat-rooms. These assembly points leave footprints in the form of huge amounts of textual data. The difficulty in obtaining insights from online user-generated content is that consumers' postings often are extremely unstructured, large in magnitude, and not easy to syndicate. Commercial (e.g., Nielsen Online) and academic text-mining tools provide marketers and researchers with an opportunity to 'listen' to consumers in the market. By doing so, firms can better understand the topics discussed, consumers' opinions, the market structure, and the competitive environment.

- **Web browsing:** The use of click-stream data, which contain click-by-click Web page-viewing information, dates back to the introduction of the Internet to the mass market. Until now the utilization of clickstream data has been limited by the inability to collect, store, and analyze the huge data sets, often in real time. However, now firms use cross-organizational skills for developing and converting these data into international market insights.

- **Social Networks and online communities:** Some of the fastest growing sources of information flow are the social-networking sites of which the most visible and powerful presences include Facebook and Twitter. Somehow consumers are turning from searching for information at news websites and search engines back to the traditional approaches of asking their friends their advice. Of course, the networking element means that they have a much wider circle of 'friends', which can also be used for more formal but 'quick-and-dirty' questionnaire surveys. Although social-networking sites have become ubiquitous, the full international marketing utilization of these sites is still untapped. The integration of social networking sites with other sources of information such as online retailers and media sources will amplify the opportunities to derive actionable marketing insights from online word-of-mouth content. Furthermore, by observing consumers' social-networking habits and purchase behavior, researches can leverage the social relationship information to identify and target opinion leaders. Furthermore, with emergence of Web 2.0, many consumer goods companies such as Nike, Harley-Davidson and Procter & Gamble have started to build their own brand communities. Brand communities open an opportunity for firms not only to enhance the interactions among consumers but to fully observe these interactions. Furthermore, brand communities open a direct of communication channel between the firm and its customer. As consumers move toward obtaining much of the information from other consumers, brand communities are likely to become a major component of the information flow.

- **Customer decision-making data:** Increasingly firms are interested not only in understanding the outcome of (or exposure to) the marketing effort but in understanding the entire process customers go though in arriving at a decision. This interest has been sparked by several technological advances in areas such as radio frequency identification (RFID), video-recognition tools and eye tracking. RFID technology allows researchers to track consumers in the retail environment, a capability to track items with the goal of improving the efficiency of supply-chain systems. Marketers can get the full picture of what is happening in the store and enable tracing consumers and product flow. The difficulty with converting these extremely valuable data into international marketing insights lies in the magnitude of data and the complexity of analysis.

- **Consumer usage data:** More and more products now are being embedded with sensors and wireless devices that can allow marketers to track consumers geographically and over time. For example, sensors on cars and consumer packaged goods can open new windows into their usage and consumption in addition to the purchase of products.

- **Neuromarketing:** Neuromarketing, referring to the use of neuroscience for marketing applications, potentially offers the ability to observe directly what consumers are thinking. Neuromarketing often is used to study brain activity to exposure to brands, product designs, or advertising. Neuromarketing is a relatively new tool for marketers, mainly owing to technological barriers, the ability to transform the neuroscience results into actionable business insights, and the high costs of collecting the data. We expect, however, that the next decade will see improvement on these fronts, making neuromarketing a common component of the customer insights tool kit.

2.4 Social Media Funnel

Social Media marketing is about using social networks and tools to guide prospect (potential) customers through a series of steps – a **funnel** – to get them to take the desired action, e.g. becoming a new customer and buying the company's product and services, with the end-goal of turning new customers into loyal customers with a high lifetime value.

As shown in Figure 2.1 (the four categories of Social Media) there are a lot of media tools. With all these Social Media marketing tools at the disposal, how should the company decide which ones fit to optimally to the social media funnel, and in which order they should be used? To answer this question, the company has to know who the potential customers are and how they can be reached most effectively. The social media marketer also has to know about the company's objectives, how it should measure these objectives (i.e. the metrics that should be analyzed) and what numbers should be set for those metrics. Figure 2.1 (below) provides a generic illustration of the social media funnel and the key metrics connected to the three stages of a typical customer buying process: Awareness, Engagement and Action.

Figure 2.1: The Social Media Funnel

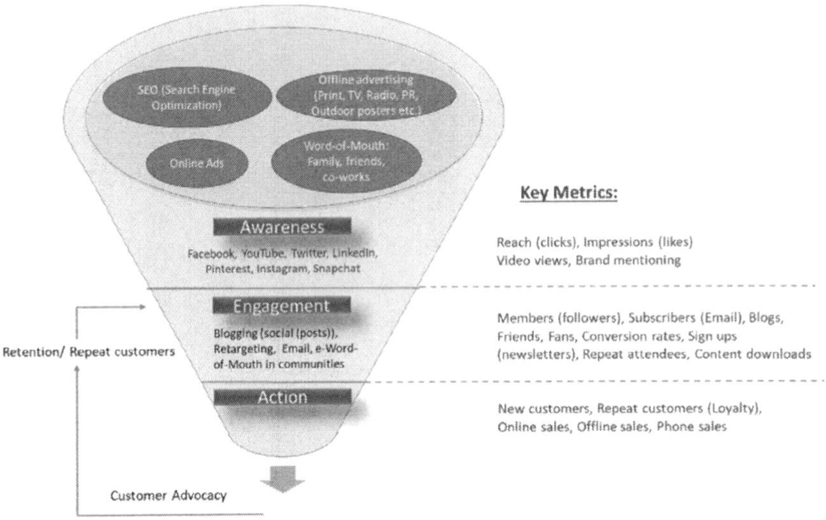

Source: Adapted from Hollensen (2019), modified

As illustrated in Figure 2.1, the following tools can act as vehicles to move and drive new potential customers into the funnel:

- SEO (Search Engine Optimization)
- Offline advertising
- Online advertising

- Word-of-Mouth conversation with family members, friends and co-workers

Any bottlenecks in the social media funnel will slow the momentum of turning prospects into actual customers or stop the process completely. Depending on where the bottleneck happens, the company could miss out on brand awareness opportunities, or conversions into actual sales.

With the key metrics in place, the company should look at each tactic in each part of the funnel and it should try and set industry benchmark standards. These benchmark standards should be used to compare the company with its competitors and the industry in general.

2.5 POE Media – Paid, Owned and Earned Media

Figure 2.2 shows how the three different digital media (paid, owned and earned media) can be combined in order to develop an effective digital marketing strategy. The figure shows the interaction and overlap between the three media types in further detail. Normally **Paid Media** are used at the top of the Marketing Funnel (see Figure 2.1.) in order to create awareness whereas **Owned Media** and **Earned Media** are used further down in the Marketing Funnel (Sciarrino et al., 2019).

Paid Media

Here the marketer pays for activities to show up in front of the audience. These are types of media that marketers can buy to create brand awareness (consider online advertising, radio, television and print.). Therefore, these media are especially good to use at the top of the Marketing Funnel (Montague, 2019).

Paid media is a great way to get an immediate return on investment. It helps the company to generate leads quickly, and it directs the audience back to the owned media where the potential customers can be nurtured and – eventually – the marketer can make a sale on them. It is also relatively easy to measure the effectiveness of the paid media, by using analytics.

The limitations to all this are that the media budget decides how fast 'scale' can be established, and conversion rates on paid media are generally lower than owned and earned media.

Figure 2.2: Digital Media Types: Paid, Owned and Earned (POE)

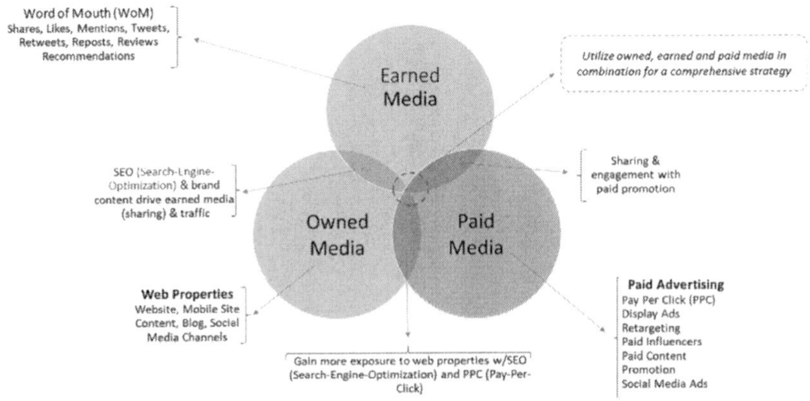

Source: Based on Tuten (2020), Sciarrino et al. (2019) and Visser et al. (2018), modified

Owned Media

These are types of media that are readily available to marketers themselves and in those they can autonomously decide on the content (for instance websites, apps, email, newsletter etc.).

With owned media, the company owns everything: the websites, blogs, and the social media accounts. The marketer is not paying for this content to show up in front of your audience, but he/she has control over all of it.

Owned media is a smart investment in any marketing strategy because it has staying power. It is possible to start a website and blogs on day one of a business and maintain it all the way until the end.

Creating owned media takes time – both in developing the content and getting it in front of the audience. It is an organic process, but it could grow and gain momentum over time.

The owned media is critical to the marketing mix because it helps the marketer building long-term relationships and earn media too.

Earned Media

These are all types of media that a brand 'earns' thanks to customers, journalists, or bloggers writing about your brand, on social media for instance, or because other organizations refer to your brand on their website. This can be anything from a press release about your business to someone talking about your products on social media.

The big benefit of earned media as part of the marketing strategy is that it is like free advertising. The business shows up in front of the audience at no cost to the marketer.

The downside to this is that the marketer does not own or control what is being put out there – which also means, that there is always a chance it can be negative PR.

How do paid, owned and earned media work together?

Now that there is an understanding of the differences of each digital media, it is important to see how to they can be combines.

The easiest way to do that is with a good example:

Let us say you have a special deal you want to publish to the social media. Instead of just pushing it organically, you pay for it to show up as an ad on that platform (Paid Media). The ad catches the attention of social media influencers and they promote it on their account, which shows up in front of even more people (Earned Media). Some of those people may then go to the company's own landing page (website) to buy the product or service. This is a perfect way to combine paid, owned and earned media for a big impact.

2.6 Customer Journey Mapping

In order to design and produce online products and services that result in a good customer experience, the entire '**customer journey**' must be viewed from the perspective of the customer. With the help of '**customer journey mapping**', the customer journey and resulting customer experience can be understood, evaluated and improved.

Customer journey mapping is a technique for optimizing customer processes and developing innovative management concepts. It identifies exactly where improvements to the customer contact processes are possible in order to achieve an optimal customer experience across all channels. It also clarifies how and what can be organized more efficiently and with greater synchronicity to give a more joined-up (seamless) customer experience. The customer journey mapping is, when used properly, an easy and effective tool for improving customer experiences across channels as well as ensuring more efficiency in customer processes.

The **customer journey map** is an indispensable tool in the designing processes of effective websites and apps. Customer journey mapping (CJM) is also a method for visualizing the purchase process or service from the customer's decision perspective (see Figure 2.3). It describes the customer's experience during the 'journey' a customer makes during the process of orientation, purchasing and eventual use of a product or service - at all points of contact and every 'touchpoint'. The customer's processing through the 'outer circle' represents the first-time buying process regarding the brand. Importantly, the conceptual model depicts a 'loyalty loop' by which customers who show post-purchase satisfaction develop brand loyalty. This would lead to future brand purchases in the 'inner circle' which would bypass some of the stages in the 'outer circle'. This provides opportunities for improvement across all channels and processes.

Figure 2.3: The Customer Journey Mapping Model

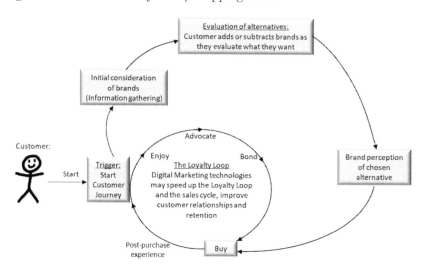

Source: Based on Edelmam and Singer (2015) and Sciarrino et al. (2019), modified

Advances in marketing technologies including marketing automation would make it possible (in Figure 2.3) for subsequent purchase journeys to accelerate, speeding up the sales cycle, improving customer retention and strengthening the customer relationship (Edelman and Singer, 2015).

Effective customer journey mapping starts from the same place as the customer starts until the point what that decision-maker considers a successful outcome.

It is important to realize that different customer segments are likely to have different customer journeys. Thus, the holiday maker's journey will look very different from the business traveller's customer journey. Someone who is actively shopping (with a deadline) may have a different journey from someone who is 'just browsing'.

2.7 Customer Touchpoint Management

Touchpoints are the individual interactions people have with brands before, during and after purchase. Marketers care about touchpoints because they represent opportunities for customers and prospects to learn, have a positive brand experience, and form attitudes and associations about the brand that could lead to future purchases, brand loyalty, and positive word-of-mouth communication.

Based on the visualization of the Customer Journey Mapping (CJM), **offline touchpoints** and **online touchpoints** can be recorded, the places where the target group and the organization meet each other (see Figure 2.4). Based on this overview, the marketer can assess whether the most cost-effective solution has been and what adjustments are needed to realize or improve the product or service.

Figure 2.4: Online and Offline Touchpoints along the Customer Journey

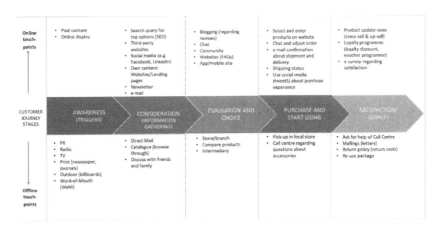

The stages and the touchpoints in the customer journey can be realized or supported via online communication media, such as websites and apps. A major advantage of online customer contact is that it allows the marketer to monitor customer behavior and with the use of advanced algorithms, elicit the most desirable response from the customer. It is possible to deliver bespoke and personalized customer experiences based on customer profiles.

This allows an organization to design and provide products that enhance customer satisfaction, bind the customer to the organization and increase customer loyalty and of course **Customer Lifetime Value (CLV)**.

Customer journey mapping including touchpoints can be applied at several different stages and for a variety of purposes (Thomke, 2019):

- Identification of market and growth opportunities from the customer's perspective
- For the organization and its employees to be able to view Digital Marketing from the perspective of the customer
- Evaluation and improvement of the realized products
- Providing direction for and keeping a handle on the process of measuring customer experiences
- Development of ideas for products and services that provide the desired customer experience
- Helping to identify that organizational changes are needed to facilitate product realization
- Development of innovative operating concepts and new services
- Gaining insight into synergy between channels

Without insight into the customer and their close involvement with the different touchpoints, a reliable customer journey analysis is not possible. An important part of this is the determination of the scope.

It is wise to determine in advance which customer segment will be investigated and what products, services, customer processes and channels are relevant.

3. Fundamentals of Social Media Marketing

3.1 The Evolution of Digital Marketing and Social Media Marketing

There is no doubt that the Internet has changed the way people communicate. For many, e-mail has virtually replaced traditional letters and even telephone calls as the choice for correspondence. Every day, billions of e-mail messages are sent out. This has also influenced the way of doing business. Against this background, media planning is undergoing a dramatic change from traditional ATL communication tools such as newspapers and magazines to non-traditional BTL tools such as mobile and Internet marketing.

Figure 3.1 displays the respective advertising market shares by medium in the years 2014 to 2019 (compared to the previous year) using the example of Germany. This is not a purely German development, but similar worldwide: since its beginnings in the mid-1990s, Internet advertising (both desktop and mobile advertising) has grown primarily at the expense of newspapers. From 2012 to 2019, global Internet advertising has risen from 18% to 39% in 2019.

This development is due to the advantages of **digital marketing**. For example, a great advantage of **"Direct E-Mail Marketing"** is that it qualifies so-called **leads**. Appropriate software allows the firm to track who is reading and responding along with the types of responses. This enables the firm to segment the audience accordingly, targeting future communications based on recipients' self-reported priorities.

A checklist for launching a successful e-mail marketing campaign includes the following aspects (Linkon, 2004):

- **Solid planning**. Companies are required to have clear and measurable objectives, and they must carefully plan their campaign.
- **Excellent content**. Standards are higher with e-mail, so firms have to make sure they are offering genuine value to the subscriber.
- **Appropriate and real 'from' field**. This is the first thing recipients look at when they are deciding whether to open an e-mail.

- **Strong 'subject' field.** The next place recipients look before deciding whether to open an e-mail is the subject field. Therefore, it needs to be compelling.

Figure 3.1: Advertising market shares of the individual media in Germany in the years 2014 to 2019 (compared to the previous year)

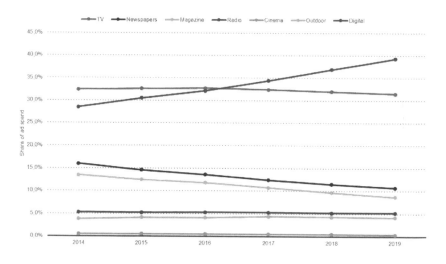

Source: www.statista.com; accessed 4th May 2020

- **Right frequency and timing.** Organizations must not overwhelm their audience. They are not supposed to send e-mail Friday through Monday or outside of normal business hours.
- **Appropriate use of graphics.** Businesses should not get carried away. If graphics add real value and aren't too big, they could be used.
- **Lead with company's strength.** Companies should not bury the best content or offer. They need to ensure it is at the top or at the e-mail equivalent of 'above the fold'.
- **Shorter is better.** Nobody reads a lot these days, and they read less in e-mail than anywhere else.

- **Personalize**. Marketers should use just three or four elements of personalization, and response rates can potentially improve by 60 per cent. They should try to go beyond just the first name and learn about the subscribers.

- **Link to company's Web site**. This is where the richness of content and interactivity can really reside. Marketers should tease readers with the e-mail so they will link to the Web site. Advertising can also be incorporated, serving the same role as the initial e-mail: to create a desire in the audience for more information. The Web site catch page is crucial to this tactic and is often where many people falter when integrating traditional advertising with online promotions.

- **Measure and improve**. The ability to measure basics such as open and click-through rates is one of the main advantages of e-mail marketing, but companies should not stop there. They should also track sales or other conversions and learn from what works and make necessary adjustments.

Web 2.0 websites allow you to do more than just retrieve information, as this was mainly the case with Web 1.0. Web 2.0 transforms broadcast media monologues (one-to-many = Web 1.0) into social media dialogues (many-to-many). The term Web 2.0 was first used in 2004 to describe a new way software developers and end-users started to utilize the internet to create content and applications that were no longer created and published by individuals, but instead continuously modified by all users in a participatory and collaborative fashion. The popularity of the term Web 2.0, along with the increasing use of blogs, wikis, and social networking technologies, has led many in academia and business to work with these 'new' phenomena. For marketers, Web 2.0 offers an opportunity to engage consumers. A growing number of marketers are using Web 2.0 tools to collaborate with consumers on product development, service enhancement and promotion. Companies can use Web 2.0 tools to improve collaboration with both its business partners and consumers. Among other things, company employees have created wikis, which are Web sites that allow users to add, delete and edit content, and to list answers to frequently asked questions about each product, and consumers have added significant contributions. Another Web 2.0 marketing feature is to make sure consumers can use the online community to network among themselves on content that they choose themselves. Besides generating content, the Web 2.0 Internet user tends to proactively bring in a whole new perspective on established processes and approaches, so that the users create innovative ideas for the future development of companies (Hollensen and Opresnik, 2015).

With the creation of the World Wide Web and Web browsers in 1990s, the Internet was transformed from a mere communication platform into a certifiably revolutionary technology. For consumers, digital technologies have not only provided the means to search for and buy products while saving time and money, but also to socialize and be entertained. The emergence of social networking sites such as MySpace and Facebook has enabled consumers to spend time socializing, and the development of video streaming and music downloads means that they can be entertained as well. A major challenge for marketers is to tap in to the huge audiences using the net.

The Internet is a global channel of communication, but the advertising messages are often perceived in the local context by the potential customer. Herein lays the dilemma that often causes the results from internet promotion to be less than anticipated.

Traditional media have two capabilities – building brands and direct marketing. In general, most promotional forms are useful for one or the other. The internet however, has the characteristics of both broadcast mass media and direct response advertising.

In the conventional model of communications in the marketplace, there are clear distinctions between the sender, the message and the recipient, and control of the message is with the sender. In 'market space', control of the message is shared between sender and receiver because of the interactivity of the medium, its ability to carry a message back in reply to that sent, and the impact of the information technology on time, space and communication. The above stated impacts on the feedback loop are built into the Internet and on the aspects of interference. In general, interference is more likely to be from internet clutter and less from external sources.

The web represents a change away from a **push strategy** in international promotion, where a producer focuses on compelling an intermediate to represent the products or services or a distributor to stock its goods, towards a **pull strategy** in which the producer communicates directly with the customer. In this transition process, promotional costs and other transaction costs are reduced. The differentiating feature of the Internet from other promotional vehicles is that of interactivity. This results in the special feature that Internet combines the attributes of both selling and advertising. Interactivity facilitates a completely innovative approach to reaching potential customers. Unlike television, for example, where the consumer passively observes, with the web there is an active intent to go onto the Internet and more attention to content as a result. In the Internet, the potential customer has a high involvement approach to advertising. A continual stream of decisions is demanded from the user. Each click represents a decision and therefore the web is a very high involvement medium. In addition, unlike traditional media, the web is a medium by which the user can click through and obtain more information or purchase the product. Web advertisements can and are often targeted to a user profile that in turn affects the way the message will be received. Increasingly, the ads displayed on the web are specific to user interests and appear as these interests are revealed while the user navigates the web. To provide value to the potential international customer and hold interest, the web site must be attractive and user friendly. This involves an appealing design, being available in the buyer's language (or one with which the buyer is likely to be familiar) and be aesthetic in terms of color and background (considering buyer's cultural norms). It should be easy to navigate, contain the information that the buyer is likely to want and be easy to access (Hollensen and Opresnik, 2015).

The most common form of advertising on the web (as opposed to advertising the existence of the web site) is banners across the top of commercial sites (Fletcher et al., 2004).

Effective Online Advertising Strategy

Marketers can use online advertising to build their brands or to attract visitors to their Web sites. Online advertising can be described as advertising that appears while customers are surfing the Web, including banner and ticker ads, interstitials, skyscrapers, and other forms. An effective advertising strategy for online advertising aims at targeting the right advertisement message to the right person at the right time (Kumar and Shah, 2004).

Who to Advertise to?

Is online advertising for everyone? Knowledgeable marketers will state that advertisement design depends on the type of product or service being sold and the desired target segment. In this respect, it is instrumental to divide the desired target segment according to first-time visitors to the company's Web site, registered users, and general information seekers. There is bound to be some overlap across these segments. However, this form of segmentation can provide useful insights while designing online advertising. Based on the user segment, the Web site can be programmed to respond appropriately. For example, every first-time visitor to a Web site can be made to see the same advertisement. Visitors identified as information seekers may be shown useful content instead of products and services directly, and registered users may see a customized advertisement message based on their profiles. Technologically, it is feasible to identify the type of user by studying their browsing behaviour through clickstream data and by using 'cookie' files.

How to Advertise?

After identifying the user or the Web site visitor, the next step is determining how to advertise or what format to use for advertising. There are several different formats of Internet advertisements: **banner ads** (which move across the screen), **skyscrapers** (tall, skinny ads at the side of a Web page) and **interstitials** (ads that pop up between changes on a Web site).

Content sponsorships are another form of Internet promotion. Many companies achieve name exposure on the Internet by sponsoring special content on various Web sites, such as news or financial information. These sponsorships are best placed in carefully targeted sites where they can offer relevant information or service to the audience. The type of advertisement chosen should be directed toward not only 'pushing' the message across but also 'pulling' the customer to click deeper into the Web site by designing ads that contribute to the overall Web site experience. For example, a Web site with too many pop-up ads on the first page runs the risk of driving the user away.

What to Advertise?

People use the Internet to seek information as well as products and services. Marketers can be creative and design advertisements that could just give out helpful information to the user. For example, a user browsing for a digital camera may be offered useful tips and pointers on how to get the best results from digital photography. Non-commercial advertising like this may not have a short-term financial gain but may contribute to superior browsing experience leading to customer loyalty and repeat visits from the user. If customer profile or history of purchase is known, it is possible to predict future purchase behaviour and companies can program buying information in the Web site code. The next time the company's Web site detects a particular user returning to the Web site, there will be an advertisement ready with an appropriate and tailored content. If deployed properly, this approach can help marketers cross-selling products through combinations of online advertisement messaging.

When to Advertise?

The first three dimensions of the advertising strategy discussed so far would be rendered ineffective if the timing is not right. In the case of offline media, one can proactively call up the customer or send him/her a direct mailer at a specific time with a customized advertising message. However, these rules do not apply online. In the case of the Internet, users may decide to go online and visit the Web site during work, in the middle of the night, or whenever they want to. Therefore, timing in the Internet context would refer to the time from the instance a user is detected online. The question is when to activate the advertisement. As soon as the user comes online, after he/she has browsed for a while, or at the time of the first purchase? Studies conducted with Internet ad timings have indicated that generally response (click-through) to pop-ups is greater when the ad appears immediately after the user enters the site. However, the results could vary greatly depending on the user segment and the user's information-seeking purposes.

Amazon.com employs a subtle form of advertisement in real time. Basically, while performing a search for a particular book, the search also throws up a list on the side or bottom of the page of relevant books that may complement the book the user was originally considering purchasing. Amazon.com was first to use 'collaborative filtering' technology, which sifts through each customer's past purchases and the purchasing patterns of customers with similar profiles to come up with personalized site content. Furthermore, the site's 'Your Recommendations' feature prepares personalized product recommendations, and its 'New for You' feature links customers through to their own personalized home pages. In perfecting the art of online selling, Amazon.com has become one of the best-known names on the Web.

Where to Advertise?

It is crucial to make Internet ads visible at vantage points to maximize their hit-rate with the intended target segment. Unlike other forms of media, where one can pick a well-defined spot within a finite set of possibilities, cyberspace offers an infinite number of possibilities across thousands of portals, search engines, and online publishers, as well as multiple possibilities within the vendor's Web site. Finding the perfect spot may seem like finding a needle in a haystack.

There are two ways to tackle this. The first is the easy way out. Follow intuition and place advertisements at obvious locations, such as frequently visited portals and search engines. However, this is not a cost-effective solution. A more refined approach involves analyzing the browsing pattern of an Internet user on a company's Web site using the Web site's log files. Analysis of the log files can help model the browsing behaviour of a random visitor to the Web site. Based on this information, Internet ad displays may be placed at appropriate locations. Marketing managers can also leverage this model to sell complementary products to potential users. For example, a department store such as Marks & Spencer may advertise cosmetics on the page where a user is buying fragrances online. An electronics store like Best Buy may advertise the latest CD releases on the page listing different audio systems.

However, this form of analysis is limited to advertising within the company's Web site. A more advanced research approach involves modelling browsing behaviour at multiple Web sites using clickstream data. Information analyzed in this manner renders a total view of a customer's online habits before purchase consideration. Such information is invaluable to marketers who would be interested in knowing when and where they're most likely to find their potential customers and, based on that information, how they should place the Internet advertisements to pull the relevant customers to their site.

Online Performance Tracking (Metrics)

Having designed an online advertising strategy, the next critical step is to track its performance. Traditional offline media (radio, television, and print advertisements) have well-defined and well-researched metrics in place that can accurately measure ad effectiveness. For example, there are many years of research testimony to show what a television commercial can do. Internet advertisements have a long way to go on this front.

Some of the most commonly used measures include:

- **click-throughs:** the number of times that users click on an advertisement
- **cost per click:** the amount spent by the advertiser to generate one click-through
- **cost per action/lead (CPA/L):** the amount spent by the advertiser to generate one lead, one desired action, or simply information on one likely user. The advertiser pays an amount based upon the number of users who fulfil the desired action.

- **cost per sale (CPS):** the amount spent by the advertiser to generate one sale. Here, the advertiser pays an amount based upon how many users actually purchase something.

Increasingly, many marketers claim to be optimizing their online campaigns using the 'cost per sale' metric, but it is clear that they are looking at sales (through online advertisements) as strictly margin transactions. The problem with this approach is that, while each individual transaction may look profitable to start with, it may not necessarily hold true over the lifetime duration of the customer. Similarly, initial returns that seem to be unprofitable may translate into very profitable transactions when measured over the lifetime value of the customer. Therefore, **Customer Lifetime Value (CLV)**, which may be defined as the measure of expected value of profit to a business derived from customer relationships from the current time to some future point, is maybe the most relevant of all metrics. It provides a direct linkage on a customer-by-customer basis to what is most important for any company-profits.

Marketing spend and outcome of advertisements guided by lifetime value measures would yield the most superior decision support system for a marketer. As companies become increasingly customer-centric, a switch to a customer lifetime value metric and building of buyer loyalty will become inevitable (Hollensen, 2006).

Building Buyer Loyalty

Using the web as a vehicle for building loyalty on the part of international buyers involves several different stages (Fletcher et al., 2004):

- **Attract:** attracting clients to visit the web site. They do so on a voluntary basis and will not come simply because a site has been created. To create awareness of the site, it is necessary to use banner ads and links to other sites
- **Engage:** engaging visitor's attention. This is necessary to get the visitor to the site to participate and encourage interaction. Most

sites fail as promotional mediums because they are boring and have poorly presented material. In this connection, the content of the site is most important.

- **Retain**: retain the visitor's interest in your site. This is important to ensure repeat visits to the site and the creation of a 'one-to-one 're-lationship between the firm and its potential overseas customer. One way of achieving this is by persuading the customer to provide information on their requirements so that the firm can customize its offering and thereby increase switching costs.

- **Learn**: learn about the client and their preferences. This is enabled by providing on the site a facility for easy feedback and comment. The use of cookies can assist.

- **Relate**: adopt a deliberate policy of building relationships with site visitors. This is achieved by providing value added content, by tailoring the product/service to the needs of each customer and promising customized delivery.

The Web as Customer Acquisition Tool

Attracting visitors to the company's website is a huge step, but it only the first. Turning them into buyers is a bigger challenge, one at which many online sellers fail. Companies lose potential customers at different stages in the purchasing process (Figure 3.2).

The stages at which customers lose interest can be summarized under the following headings:

- home page
- product search
- after product found
- shopping cart
- failure to repeat purchase

A reason for defection which applies throughout each of these stages is unacceptable download times.

Figure 3.2: Internet buying behaviour

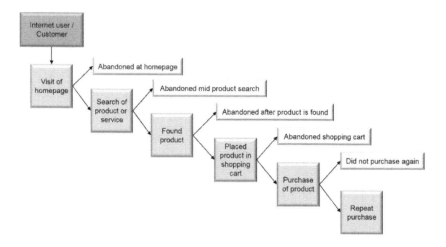

Source: Adapted from Hollensen and Opresnik (2015), modified

We will now look at each of these stages in turn (Hollensen and Opresnik, 2015):

- **Abandoned at home page**
  There are many reasons why a visitor may take one look at a company's home page and decide to leave. Errant advertising is a leading cause. Established clicks-and-mortar companies have an advantage over pure-plays in attracting visitors. People know from experience what the company sells. But even well-established brands can lose a significant percentage of their homepage visitors. Often, it is poor design features such as time-consuming download time or confusing navigation that drive them away.

- **Abandoned mid product search**

  Customers who leave the website while they're still perusing merchandise typically do so when they can't find what they're looking for. Perhaps the selection is too narrow, or the shopper has run out of gift ideas. Best-practice merchants overcome such problems by feeding the visitor suggestions ('We think you'll also love ...'), directing them to the recipient's wish list.

- **Abandoned after product is found**

  Even after online customers find what they are looking for, many stop short of making a purchase. There are numerous reasons: For example, net shoppers who decide not to purchase holiday gifts online may want to actually see the physical product before buying it. Small pictures and incomplete product information keep many browsers from buying online. Out-of-stock items and high prices are also deterrents. To stem the tide of customer defections at this stage of the buying process, some online merchants such as Lands End offer a live chat feature so shoppers can get their questions answered on the spot.

- **Abandoned shopping cart**

  The foremost reason customers abort an online shopping trip is a cumbersome checkout process. Other reasons include excessive shipping costs and concerns about credit-card security or making returns. In this final moment of weighing up, multi-channel companies whose offline business has already established a strong brand and loyal customers are less likely to lose out on the sale. Retailers must have an efficient checkout process that minimizes the amount of information shoppers have to enter and closes the sale as quickly as possible.

- **Failure to repeat purchase**

  A repeat customer is likely to be more favorable than a new customer since repeat shoppers tend to spend more. One of the main reasons why customers do not return is delivery problems. As the customer expectations are very high in this regard online marketers must make or buy a back-end system that will meet or exceed customer needs. Managing customer expectations is also important. In the case of stock outs or backorders, it is better to give shoppers the bad news before they submit an order than to send a follow-up e-mail, as some e-retailers do. While the result may be a lost sale, preserving the customer relationship is more profitable in the long run.

- **Unacceptable download times**

  Another factor in customer abandonment that is relevant at all points in the transaction chain is slow download and server response times. Five seconds is considered a 'breaking point' for page downloads, above which customers will go elsewhere. Meanwhile, consumer expectations are continually mounting. Companies that decline to make the necessary investments to keep their websites fast may see declines in sales and retention. But companies should be cautious how they invest in their sites; fancy graphics and inter-activity features designed to simplify the purchase process can actually slow down transaction times, especially since many potential customers do not have high bandwidth. Even if the servers are adequate, a data-rich website (such as one with lots of images, flash capabilities, or sound) may render your site maddeningly slow and impractical for a large percentage of your potential customers. The key for retailers is to find the balance between the site's marketing impact, its functionality, and the ability of company and consumer infrastructure to handle the content.

3.2 Definition of Social Media Marketing

Social media are Internet-based technologies that facilitate online conversations and encompass a wide range of online, word-of-mouth forums including social networking websites, blogs, company sponsored discussion boards and chat rooms, consumer-to-consumer e-mail, consumer product or service ratings websites and forums, Internet discussion boards and forums, and sites containing digital audio, images, movies, or photographs, to name a few. Since 2009, the official company and brand web sites have typically been losing audience. This decline is believed to be due to the emergence of social media marketing by the brands themselves, an increasingly pervasive marketing practice. According to ebizmba.com the world's largest social networking site is Facebook, which was initially founded by Mark Zuckerberg in order to stay in touch with his fellow students from Harvard University.

Figure 3.3 lists the ten most popular social networking sites per March 2020.

Figure 3.3: Social Media, World Top 10 per March 2020

Social Media	Country	Comments	Active users per month
1. Facebook	US	In 2018 Facebook came under attack for allowing 3rd parties to access millions of users' personal data	1,600 million
2. WhatsApp	US	Acquired by Facebook in 2014. Give users ability to communicate and share instantly with individuals and groups	1,000 million
3. QQ	China	Tencent owned. Instant messaging (chat-based). It became international, after it was launched in China	860 million
4. WeChat	China	Tencent owned. All-in-one communication app, plus gaming. Growing fast	700 million
5. QZone	China	Tencent owned. Enabling share of photos, watch videos, listen to songs, write blogs, maintain diaries etc.	650 million
6. Tumblr	US	Owned by Yahoo since 2013. A micro blogging platform where users can post anything including multimedia	550 million
7. TikTok	China	Owned by ByteDance. Initially launched as Douyin in September 2016. The app allows the user to create short music videos. Especially popular among teenagers.	500 million
8. Instagram	US	Owned by Facebook. Based on sharing photos and videos	450 million
9. Twitter	US	Enabling posts of short text messages (called tweets), containing limited number of characters (up to 280)	330 million
10. Baidu Tieba	China	Owned by Baidu, a search engine. Allow users to create a social network group for a specific topic	300 million

Source: Based on www.makeawebsitehub.com/social-media-sites/ and Statista.com

The Chinese social media sites such as QZone and Weibo Tieba are mainly active in their home country. In the West, it is possible to get away with a two-way platform strategy consisting of Facebook and Google. However, in China, there are not only social media platforms that do not exist elsewhere in the world, but there are also multiple overlapping platforms and ecosystems that are in constant movement. For example, WeChat is the go-to platform not only for chatting and e-commerce transactions, but also for P2P transfer, bill payment and even mutual fund investment. For an outsider, an environment like this requires persistent monitoring to understand, plan and execute for maximum impact of the Chinese customers. For social media usage and development, the diversity of languages is creating communication challenges on a global basis. Facebook has 1,100 million weekly users, with more than 70% outside the United States. To effectively communicate with non-English users, Facebook has 70 translations available on its site made possible by a vast network of 300,000 volunteers and translators. Facebook and Twitter offer direct selling companies means of communicating with key stakeholders (customers and distributors) in the industry. On the other hand, YouTube, with its more traditional one-way audience communication, appears to be used more effectively for recruiting consumers to become distributors of information or products. One of the 'shooting stars' during the last years is LinkedIn, which is a social networking website for people in professional occupations. Launched in 2003, it is mainly used for professional networking. While Facebook, YouTube, and Twitter continue to dominate social media in the US and Europe some other countries, the global scene tells a different story. In Germany, Russia, China (see above) and Japan, the most visited social networking site is not Facebook but home-grown rivals.

We will look at the most important Multi-Platform Social-Networking Websites & Forums for marketers in more depth in later chapters of this book.

3.3 From ‚Bowling‘ to ‚Pinball‘

Integrated marketing communications (IMC) have traditionally been considered to be largely one-way in nature ('bowling' – see below Figure 3.4).

In the old paradigm, the organization and its agents developed the message and transmitted it to potential consumers, who may or may not have been willing participants in the communication process. The control over the dissemination of information was in the hands of the firm's marketing organization. The traditional elements of the promotion mix (advertising, personal selling, public relations and publicity, direct marketing and sales promotion) were the tools through which control was asserted.

The twenty-first century is witnessing an explosion of Internet-based messages transmitted through these media. They have become a major factor in influencing various aspects of consumer behaviour including awareness, information acquisition, opinions, attitudes, purchase behaviour and post-purchase communication and evaluation. Unfortunately, the popular business press and academic literature offers marketing managers very little guidance for incorporating social media into their IMC strategies (Hollensen and Opresnik, 2015).

Social networking as communication tools has two interrelated promotional roles:

- **Social networking should be consistent with the use of traditional IMC tools.** That is, companies should use social media to talk to their customers through such platforms as blogs, as well as Facebook and Twitter groups. These media may either be company-sponsored or sponsored by other individuals or organizations.
- **Social networking is enabling customers to talk to one another.** This is an extension of traditional word-of-mouth communication. While companies cannot directly control such consumer-to-consumer (C2C) messages, they do can influence the conversations that consumers have with one another. However, consumers' ability to communicate with one another limits the amount of control companies have over the content and dissemination of information. Consumers are in control; they have greater access to information and greater command over media consumption than ever before.

Marketing managers are seeking ways to incorporate social media into their IMC strategies. The traditional communications paradigm, which relied on the classic promotional mix to craft IMC strategies, must give way to a new paradigm that includes all forms of social media as potential tools in designing and implementing IMC strategies. Contemporary marketers cannot ignore the phenomenon of social media, where available market information is based on the experiences of individual consumers and is channeled through the traditional promotion mix. However, various social media platforms, many of which are completely independent of the producing/sponsoring organization or its agents, enhance consumers' ability to communicate with one another.

Although a little oversimplified, marketing in the pre-social media era was comparable to 'bowling' (see Figure 3.4).

Figure 3.4: The Bowling to Pinball model: Transition of market communication from 'bowling' to 'Pinball'

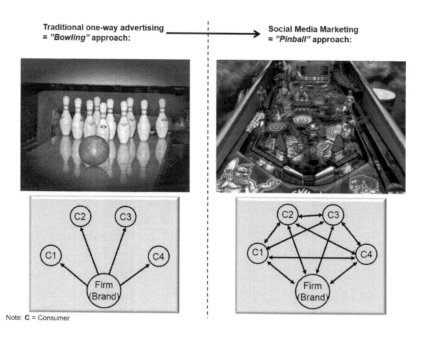

Source: Adapted from Hollensen and Opresnik (2015), modified

A game of bowling shows how you may have traditionally communicated with your consumers, with the firm and the brand (the bowler) rolling a ball (the brand communication message) towards the pins (our target customers). Clearly this is a very direct one-way communication approach. This is the old traditional push model. Marketers targeted certain customer groups and sent out their advertising messages like precisely bowled bowling balls. They used traditional media to hit as many bowling pins as possible. One key characteristic of this bowling marketing game was the large amount of control the company retained over marketing communication because consumers were given only limited freedom of action. For many bigger companies a large TV-budget has been the ball that marketers rolled down the lane, trying to hit as many the pins as possible. Marketers were in control, happily counting how many 'pins' they had hit, and how often. Success in this game was clear-cut, and the metrics clear (Hennig-Thurau et. al., 2013).

In a social media marketing world, the bowling metaphor does not fit anymore. On this arena, marketing can be better described as playing 'Pinball': Companies serve up a 'marketing ball' (brands and brand-building messages) into a dynamic and chaotic market environment. The 'marketing ball' is then diverted and often accelerated by social media 'bumpers', which change the ball's course in chaotic ways. After the marketing ball is in play, marketing managers may continue to guide it with agile use of the 'flippers' but the ball does not always go where it is intended to. Consequently, in the 'pinball' world, you cannot know outcomes in advance. Instead, marketers have to be prepared to respond in real time to the spin put on the ball by consumers. When mastered well, the pinball game can deliver big point multipliers, and if the company is very good, even more balls can be shot into the game. A reason for this may be that today consumers have a large audience to bring up new topics on the communication agenda. In the ideal situation, you are reaching networked influencers, advocates, and other high-value consumers, who may sustain and spread positive conversations about the brand across multiple channels. Occasionally, the marketing ball will come back to the company. At this point, the firm (brand) has to use the flippers to interact and throw it back into the social media sphere. If the company or the brand do not feed the social marketing media sphere by flipping communications back, the ball will finally drop through the flippers and on longer term, the two-way relationship between consumers and the firm (brand) will die (Hollensen and Opresnik, 2015).

3.4 The Extended Model of Social Media Marketing Communication

The 'Bowling to Pinball' model can be further elaborated into an extended model of interactive market communication (Hollensen and Opresnik, 2015).

The four different communication styles, represented in Figure 3.5 are:

- **The Traditional one-way advertising** (mass media advertising like television advertising, newspaper / magazine advertising etc.) represents the 'bowling' approach where the firm attempts to 'hit' as many customers with 'shotgun' mass media methods. Normally this approach is a one-way communication type.

- **Customer-driven interaction** represents a higher degree of interaction between the company and its different key customers. Often the company finds some Key Account managers, who have the responsibility of taking care of the one-to-one interaction between the firm and its key accounts (customers).

- **Viral Marketing** is representing the version 1.0 of Social Media Marketing, where the company e.g. uses an untraditional YouTube video to get attention and awareness about its brand. The interaction between the potential 'customers' is quite high (blogging sites etc.), but the feed-back to the company is relatively low (no double arrows back to the company).

- **Social Media Marketing** is representing the version 2.0 of Social Media Marketing, where there is also an extensive feed-back to the company itself (double arrows back to the company). Here the company proactively has chosen to be a co-player in the discussion and blogging on the different relevant social media sites (Facebook, Twitter etc.). This also means that the company here tries to strengthen the interaction with the customers in a positive direction, in order to influence the customer behavior. To do so, the company needs a back-up team of social media employees who can interact and communicate on-line with potential and actual customers. Consequently, this strategy is also very resource demanding.

Figure 3.5: The extended interactive market communication model'

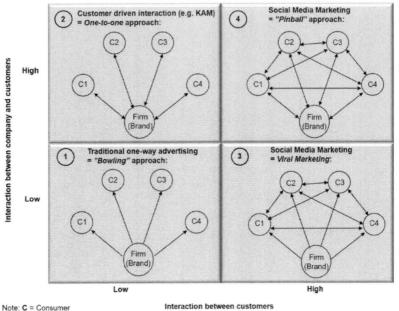

Note: C = Consumer   Interaction between customers

Source: Adapted from Hollensen and Opresnik (2015), modified

3.5 The 6C Model of Social Media Marketing

The social media (e.g. Facebook or Twitter) are essentially vehicles for carrying content. This content – in form of words, text, pictures and videos – is generated by millions of potential customers around the world, and from your perspective (= company's perspective) this can indeed be an inspiration to create further value for these customers. The following model (Hollensen and Opresnik, 2015) mainly represents alternative 4 in Figure 3.5. If there had been no feed-back to the company in the model, it would have been more like alternative 3. Figure 3.6 defines six distinct, interrelated elements (Cs) that explain the creation and retention of consumer engagement, seen from a company perspective; however, the user-generated contents still plays an important role in the model.:

- **Company and contents:** The 6C model begins with the company and the content it creates. Basically, the Internet remains a 'pull' medium, in the way that firms seek to pull viewers to its content, and finally to the company itself. However, before any 'pull' can happen, the content has to be pushed (seeded) forward in the chain. Content can take the form of e.g. a Facebook product or brand page, and/or a YouTube video pushed out to viewers. Consequently, content pushed into the social media sphere by a company acts as a catalyst for our model of engagement or participation.

Figure 3.6: The 6C model (Company, Contents, Control, Community, Consumers, Conversation)

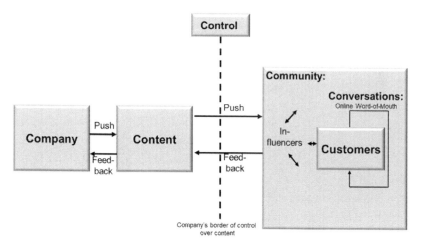

Source: Adapted from Hollensen (2019), modified

- **Control:** The dashed line denoting control in the 6C model (Figure 3.6) is intended to represent a wall beyond which the company let over control of its brand to the online community and the customers. To accelerate the viral uptake of its brand messaging, the company sometimes gives up the digital rights and blocks in order to encourage online community members to copy, modify, re-post, and forward the content. The content is intended to be copied and/or embedded into people's websites, blogs, and on Facebook walls. The key point to this stage in the process is that the company (the content creator) must be willing, and even embrace, the fact that they no longer have full control over the content: it is free to be taken, modified, commented on, and otherwise appropriated by the community of interest. This may challenge the conventional 'brand management' wisdom stating that managers must keep control of brand image and messaging.

- **Community:** The company creates content and pushes it over the symbolic border of control to the other side, where a community of interested consumers now takes it up. At this point, communication becomes bidirectional. The use of arrows in Figure 3.6 for push and pull, attempts to reflect the 'give-and-take' that goes on between a community and the company, represented by the content creators. In its simplest form, it is reflected in the art of commenting: posting reactions, on Facebook or YouTube, to the content. In some cases, the company can even lean about 'customer behaviour' in the market by following these online community discussions. In an ideal world, a series of reflexive conversations take place in the community, independent of any action by the company, which will often have a passive role as an observer.

  When transferring the 'content' into the online community, the company and the content providers often try to target the '**Influencers**', which are defined as individuals who have access to a large amount of marketplace information, and proactively engage in discussions with other online community members and customers to diffuse and spread this content.

  Influencers are typically the first to receive the message and transmit it to their immediate social networks. They function as connectors or bridges between different subcultures and their network of social hubs can facilitate immediate transmission of the content to thousands of online community members.

- **Customers and conversations:** The ultimate expression of engagement occurs when a multitude of online conversations circle around the phenomenon and content, as illustrated above and in Figure 3.6. The 6C model distinguishes between the online community and potential customers, as the latter are usually a subset of the former. The online community may also include people who have heard of the Web-based initiative but not directly participated in it.

  In general, there seems to be a growing escalation in participation on the part of customers; a willingness to engage with a brand that extends beyond just purchase decisions at the point of sale.

According to the 6C model, Social media further extend the conversations between marketers and consumers through a feedback loop, which might happen after some on-line conversation (blogging etc.) in the community. After some time of online conversation, the company may have chats with the online community in hopes of influencing purchase decisions. Moreover, social media initiatives provide marketers a glimpse into the world of customer-to-customer communication, which represents a significant extension of the more traditional advertising and word-of-mouth communication.

Furthermore, social media provide insights into the behavior of non-customers. Most social media marketers try to trigger buzz among prospective customers. This has led to social sharing whereby online community member broadcast their thoughts and activities to strangers all over the world. This social sharing has opened the lives of individual consumers that companies can then exploit to tailor their offerings to better match preferences (Hollensen and Opresnik, 2015).

3.6 Influencer Marketing

When transferring the 'content' into the online community, the company and the content providers often try to target the influencers (or opinion leaders), which are typically some of the first to receive the message and transmit it to their immediate social networks. They function as connectors or bridges between different subcultures, and their network of social hubs can facilitate immediate transmission of the content to thousands of online community members.

The broad group of influencers can be characterized into the following groups (ANA, 2018):

Micro-Influencers:	50 – 25,000 followers
Macro-Influencers:	25,001 – 100,000 followers
Mega-Influencers	100,001 – 500,000 followers
Celebrity-Influencers	Over 500,000 followers

The purpose with 'Influencer Marketing' is to win customer trust, especially when compared to traditional online ads. Influencer Marketing is less intrusive and more flexible than traditional online ads. An **influencer** is an individual who proactively engage in discussions with other online community members and customers to diffuse and spread this content. It can be a teenage girl posting about her favorite local ice-cream bar to make a few bucks, or it can be a celebrity-influencer like Kim Kardashian posting about a clothing line to make $200,000.

For SMEs it is absolutely relevant to work with **micro-influencers**, who are individuals who work in their special category and are truly knowledgeable, passionate and authentic. They are seen as a trusted source when it comes to recommendations for what to buy. Micro-influencers are affecting a much smaller social circle (segments) around them, but they can do it much more effective than mega- or celebrity influencers. Haenlein and Libai (2018) showed that micro-influencers not only have over 20 times more conversations with their social group than an average consumer, but they also found that 80% of potential customers are very likely to follow their recommendations. Marketers therefore do not have to turn to celebrities to enhance their social media campaigns.

3.7 Global Smartphone Marketing

Smartphone marketing, mobile marketing or **M-marketing** should be considered within the context of m-business and m-commerce. Emerging from recent developments in communications technology, m-business represents 'mobile' business and 'refers to the new communications and information delivery model created when telecommunications and the Internet converge'.

Together with the widespread adoption of 4G (and in the future 5G) smartphones among consumers, mobile marketing has increasingly become an important tool in brands' international advertising and promotional efforts.

The next generation of the internet standard in mobile marketing (m-marketing) will allow programs to run through a web browser rather than a specific operating system. That means consumers will be able to access the same programs and cloud-based content from any device – personal computer, laptop, smartphone or tablet – because the browser is the common platform. This ability to work seamlessly anytime, anywhere, on any device could change consumer behaviour and shift the balance of power in the distribution systems towards the end of the distribution system – the end-buyer, who has cheaper and cheaper access to the new mobile devices. It will create opportunities for marketers to distribute goods and services more directly to the end-buyers and it will present increasing challenges for the intermediaries between the manufacturers and the end-buyers (Hollensen and Opresnik, 2015).

Rapidly emerging innovations have also delivered the possibility of smartphones able to use product bar codes to access product-related information and phones able to act as e-wallets, as either a prepaid card for small purchases or a fully functioning credit/debit card unit.

However, the mobile industry will also see a lot more enforcement on the mobile security and privacy in the coming years, as many questions have been raised regarding mobile payments, coupons and applications. Mobile commerce is on the rise, which means people are more comfortable with the idea of paying with their phones. However, there is still a critical view throughout the mobilized world regarding the safety of this kind of payment system.

Benefits of M-Marketing

The introduction of m-marketing should bring a series of benefits to consumers, merchants and telecommunication companies. As with all technologies, many benefits will arise in the future that have not yet even been imagined.

Some benefits that are apparent now, however, include the following:

For consumers

- **Comparison shopping.** Consumers can access on demand, at the point of purchase, the best prices in the marketplace. This can be done now without mobility, with services such as pricescan.com.
- **Bridge the gap between bricks and clicks.** Services permitting users to examine merchandise in a store and still shop electronically for the best price.
- **Opt-in searches.** Customers may receive alerts from merchants when products they are looking for become available.
- **Travel.** Ability to change and monitor scheduled travel any time, any place.

For merchants

- **Impulse buying.** Consumers may buy discounted products from a web page promotion
  or a mobile alert, increasing their willingness to buy when they are near or even inside the store, thus increasing merchants' sales.
- **Drive traffic.** Companies will guide their customers to where it is easier to carry out the transaction, to either online or offline stores, due to the time-sensitive, location-based and personalized characteristics of the mobile device.
- **Education of consumers.** Companies will send information to customers about product benefits or new products.
- **Perishable products.** This is especially important for products that do not retain their value when unused, such as service-based

products. For example, the use of an airplane seat, which, when unused, generates no revenue and is lost value. This will enable companies to manage inventory more effectively.

- **Drive efficiency.** Companies will save time with their clients. Because information is readily available on the mobile device, they will not have to talk about the benefits of the different products or about prices.
- **Target market.** Companies will be better able to target their products to those in each geographic area at a specific time.

For telecommunication companies, the advantages are primarily more airtime used by the consumers and higher fees charged to content providers for each m-commerce transaction. M-marketing requires direct marketers to rethink their strategies to tap into already existing communities – such as sports fans, surfers and music fans; time-context communities such as spectators at sports events and festivals; and location-sensitive communities such as gallery visitors and small shoppers – and develop ways to get them to opt in to m-marketing. Applications must be responsive to location, customer needs and device capabilities. For example, time- and location-sensitive applications, such as travel reservations, cinema tickets and banking, will be excellent vehicles for young, busy, urban people. Finally, as highlighted, m-marketing enables distribution of information to the consumer at the most effective time, place and in the right context. This suggests that m-marketing, via mobile devices, will cement further the interactive marketing relationship. Smartphones are a vital piece of technology, as their owners take them wherever they go and they can be used to deliver a message based on consumers' shopping preferences just before the point of purchase (Dube and Helkkula, 2015).

3.8 Global App Marketing

In January 2020, 2.57 million Android apps and 1.84 million Apple apps were available. On average, smartphone users have around 40 apps on their mobile phones and regularly use around 15.

Apps offer companies a wide range of revenue opportunities. Global app revenue in 2017 was approximately $82 billion and is estimated to exceed $139 billion in 2021. As free apps become increasingly prevalent, paid app downloads are expected to decline, and advertising and in-app purchases are likely to become the main revenue streams in the coming years. With the rise in smartphones and tablets across the globe, the mobile app industry has been rapidly growing. Mobile advertising has seen triple-digit percentage growth each year since 2010.

Mobile apps can be classified into **mobile commerce** and **mobile value-added services (MVAS)**, see also the mobile app spectrum in Figure 3.7):

- **Mobile commerce:** Here the app mostly has the purpose of selling a product or a service. For example, the Domino's Pizza app is designed to generate sales and promote special deals to customers.
- **Mobile value-added services (MVAS):** Here the app offers services that are not directly tied to sales but are designed to help customers solve problems or make decisions. Such an app enriches the total customer experience of a product offering.

An example of an MVAS is an airline app that can be used to generate a mobile boarding pass (QR code) in a co-production process between the airline and the customer. Conceptually, the core service (the flight) and the MVAS (mobile boarding pass) need to be interrelated constructs building the final customer experience - flight from A to B. Similarly, the **Makeup Genius** app from L'Oréal can be seen as assisting the user in selecting the best make-up to build the final service ('looking good and attractive').

Exhibit 3.1

L'Oréal is extending the customers' buying experience with the mobile app Makeup Genius - Digitalization is reinventing the rules of the game in the beauty industry.

Many beauty stores experience that people have unwrapped products in the shops, because they don't carry testers, and many women feel that buying makeup without trying it is risky. The art of purchasing drugstore cosmetics is wildly imperfect. Women are expected to choose a foundation by comparing the color of the bottle to the color of your arm and to spend $10 on a lipstick after holding it next to your face in front of a tiny mirror.

Figure 3.7 The Mobile App spectrum

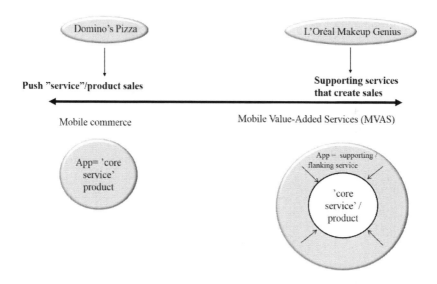

Source: Based on Hollensen (2017), p. 543, modified

L'Oréal, the French beauty giant, thinks there's a better way. In June 2014, the company released the *Makeup Genius*, an app that lets the woman see herself in real time wearing products that are not actually on her face. When she smiles, pucker up, or wink, the virtual cosmetics move along with her. She can apply, say, a lip liner with a lipstick or choose from full looks such as Evening Smokey and Jennifer's Nude (as in J. Lo), created with a bundle of products. Although there were already many make-up apps out there, these were based on users taking photos of themselves and then applying make-up to the still image.

For L'Oréal, the Makeup Genius app is an alternative to consumers going into a store to try out cosmetics. Their consumers can try out the products they might not otherwise have tested or considered. This used to be impossible since the manufacturers earlier had to rely on retailers to interact directly with consumers.

This is how the woman (or man) can get the Makeup Genius to work:

- Download the Makeup Genius app on the IOS or Android smartphone or table
- Take a selfie. The app uses a facial mapping technology that shows the user what the make-up looks like on her/his face as she/he moves or smiles into the virtual mirror of the phone's camera. The virtual make-up follows the face movements.

Make-up products (limited to L'Oréal's product range) can be tried out virtually at the touch of a button. The app allows the user to save the results of these virtual makeovers and share them with friends on social media or via e-mail. The app also features different looks from make-up artists – some of them modelled by L'Oréal brand ambassadors such as Freido Pinto.

Once decided, the user can buy the cosmetic products online directly from L'Oréal. A barcode scanner means that she shopper can also try the products virtually in stores too.

Guive Balooch has a Ph.D. in biomaterials and came up with the idea for Makeup Genius together with a fellow biologist during a brainstorming session in 2012. At the time, several cosmetics companies, including L'Oréal, were offering virtual makeup counters on their websites and at drugstores, but most required users to upload a picture and Photoshop lipstick and eye shadow onto the static image—a time-consuming process. Guive Balooch and his Balooch's tech lab (now with 15 engineers and scientists) developed the app for L'Oréal.

Balooch's team tested eye, lip, and cheeked products on hundreds of models with varying complexions, capturing how each shade and texture transforms under 400 different lighting conditions. The company also collected more than 100,000 images to compare how the makeup looks on the models in real life vs. on-screen.

During development, L'Oréal worked together with Image Metrics, a creator of facial recognition software for video games and movies, including 2008's *The Curious Case of Benjamin Button*, in which the title character, played by Brad Pitt, ages in reverse.

Of course, L'Oréal hopes all that the Makeup Genius will lead to more purchases, either through its built-in e-commerce platform or at a local store. Now around 16% of L'Oréal's media budget go to digital media, but the results are also coming up. Alone in 2014, the L'Oréal e-commerce beauty sales increased with 20%, up to €800 million. By the end of 2015 the app had been downloaded app. 15 million times.

Source: Based on Korporaal (2015) and Daneshkhu (2014)

Another MVAS app is **Kraft Foods** that offers an **iFood** Assistant app, which allows users to browse recipes by occasion or category and then add the necessary ingredients to a shopping list. It includes a recipe box option that lets users access favorite recipes.

On the spectrum from mobile commerce to mobile services (MVAS), many apps offer on-the-go services paired with location-based technology. Companies employ technology for both geocoding (based on location latitude and longitude) and reverse geocoding (translating coordinates into a street address) to deliver accurate locations. One example of a location-based app is the **Tinder** dating app, which is a social discovery application that facilitates communication between mutually interested users. The Tinder 'matchmaking' app is based on criteria like geographical location, number of mutual friends, and common interests. Based on these criteria the app then makes a list of geographical near-by potential candidates. The app then allows the user to anonymously like another user by swiping right or pass by swiping left on them. If two users like each other it then results in a 'match' and they are then able to chat within the app.

Summing up, developing an effective mobile marketing program is much more challenging than developing a traditional program aimed at laptop and desktop users. The mobile program needs to be planned, implemented, and tested for multiple devices (smartphones, tablets, laptops, and desktops) and different operating systems, and should adjust for the limitations of mobile devices in terms of screen and traditional keyboard size. In addition, the immediacy, location, and personalization attributes of mobile devices increase the need to develop a portfolio of messages to reflect such attributes as weather conditions (immediacy), distance to a store (location), and a consumer's preferences and past purchase behavior (personalization).

3.9 e-Services and 'Cloud Computing'

Due to the continuing expansion of the internet, consumer behaviour has changed and new needs have emerged. As an interactive medium, the internet combines the best of mass production (based on the manufacture of products) and customization (typically found in services). The ultimate tool for mass customizing can treat each customer as being unique. Enterprises devoted to combining new technologies with traditional service concepts have created a new type of services called **e-services**. E-services deliver intangible information-based products and services through interaction with online users. Basically, an e-service can be defined as a business activity of value exchange that is accessible through electronic networks, which include the internet and mobile networks. It involves distributing and personalizing resources in real-time over the internet.

The e-services include services that use only the internet as the user interface and situations where the actual service fulfilment might include non-electronic channels (e.g. shopping), as well as services that are entirely delivered electronically (e.g. music streaming and download).

Currently, services delivered over the internet offer entirely new opportunities in the era of the digital economy. E-service has become increasingly significant, not only for determining the success or failure of e-commerce ventures but by delivering a superior overall experience for customers. The emergence of the internet regarding services has enhanced cost benefits for enterprises, as well as the speed, efficiency and flexibility of online transactions. Furthermore, this unique approach to delivering services provides a novel experience and alters customer expectations.

Development of new e-service offerings takes place in many industries, such as financial services, health care, telecommunications services, leisure and hospitality services, information services, legal and educational services, and many more. Development of new e-services stresses core differences between products and services: intangibility, heterogeneity and simultaneity.

In the simplest terms, **cloud computing** means storing and accessing data and programs over the Internet instead of your computer's hard drive. The cloud is just a metaphor for the Internet.

The innovations in cloud computing result from its ability to share information resources in a self-service fashion with little interaction from the Internet service provider. Information can be accessed from any location or device, which provides better utilization of a consumer's digital information. For consumers, the ability to access information at any time or geographic location has resulted in better access to marketing information that was previously expensive and difficult to obtain. This aspect of 'cloud computing' is of course important from a global marketing perspective (Ratten, 2015).

For international marketers, cloud computing provides global access to computing resources that can be reconfigured based on international location. As more companies and consumers are working in the international business world, cloud computing provides a cheaper and better alternative to traditional information technology data storage and access services.

Cloud computing has changed the way business apps are developed and deployed. Companies no longer need to buy and maintain their own infrastructure of servers, storage and development tools to create and run business apps. Instead, companies can gain access to a variety of business apps via an Internet browser or mobile device on an as-needed basis, without the cost and complexity of managing the hardware or software in-house.

The broad shift to social networking has transformed the way people collaborate and is accelerating the adoption of technologies that connect people and products through 'feeds' and status updates. There is a significant transition underway from desktops to smartphones and tablets, making it possible for people to get business done right from their mobile devices. And increasingly, customers want to be connected to the products they use.

61

The worldwide demand for cloud computing services is expected to record strong growth in coming years. Cloud computing is a computing infrastructure model, which enables delivery of software-as-a-service (SaaS). Appeal to cloud computing has been increasing as it enables the companies to reduce expenses like upfront royalty or licensing payments, investment in hardware infrastructure and other operating expenses. One company that is in forefront on 'cloud' CRM solutions is Salesforce.com – see Exhibit 3.2

Exhibit 3.2

Salesforce.com as provider of CRM 'cloud' services

Salesforce.com founded on the concept of delivering CRM applications via the Internet, or 'cloud.' They introduced their first CRM solution in February 2000 and they have expanded our offerings with new editions, solutions and enhanced features, through internal development and acquisitions. Their mission is to help our customers transform themselves into 'customer companies' by empowering them to connect with their customers in entirely new ways. Salesforce.com derives their revenues primarily from subscription fees (one year at a time) for their services. In fiscal 2017, Salesforce.com generated revenue of $8.39 billion. Approximately 30 percent of their revenue comes from customers outside of the Americas (North and South America). On January 1, 2018, Salesforce.com had 25,000 employees. Growing demand for cloud CRM software services will facilitate the company's revenue and market share growth in coming years. However, Salesforce.com operates in the CRM solutions market, which is highly competitive, rapidly evolving and fragmented. The company primarily competes with vendors of packaged business software and companies offering CRM apps. Salesforce.com also faces competition from internally developed applications. The major direct competitors of the company include Microsoft, NetSuite, Oracle, and SAP.

Source: Based on Salesforce.com and other public sources

4. Digital and Social Media Marketing Tools and Platforms

4.1 A Systemizing Social Media Framework

Social media employs mobile and Web- based technologies to share, co-create, discuss, and modify user-generated content. It has transformed the traditional marketing communication model - which was primarily a one-way communication from the marketer to customers. This has shifted to a model with much more feedback flowing in the opposite direction and this has created a paradigm shift. Not only are consumers more in command of the communication flowing toward them, but they can also initiate communication directed toward marketers. Further, interaction between customers has increased dramatically.

The marketplace has changed, and marketers' thinking must evolve accordingly. Consumers now share information across a plethora of social media platforms at an unpredictable pace that is hardly under the marketer's influence. Communication created by consumers will also affect how markets are targeted and how products will be created and delivered. The philosophy of satisfying customers' needs and wants will gain increasing prominence across all marketing activities as consumers continue to gain control, learn to use social media to their advantage, and expect to get exactly what they want. More active consumer involvement will also lead to more transparency in branding, so delivering quality will be a necessity. Brand managers stuck in the old paradigm will experience extreme difficulties, handicapped by their limited ability to respond to consumer preferences. Social media democratized this process with a much wider participation and the power to elevate the brand, provided the product is good.

Today's stamp of quality assurance is word-of-mouth of social media participants. Niches can now thrive because small groups of consumers can spread the word to others who may also want the brands they like (Kohli et al, 2015).

The Social Media tools and platforms will be organized around Tuten and Solomon's (2015) **four zones of social media** (Figure 4.1). It is a way to focus on the most important functions of each social media platform. The various uses of social media for personal and commercial purposes often mean some overlap of more zones e. g. as the case with Facebook or Snapchat. That is the nature of social media. All social media are networked around relationships, technologically enabled, and based on the principles of shared participation.

In the following sections of the book, we are going to describe the different zones and the most important respective social media platforms and websites in more detail.

4.2 Social Community Zone

Zone 1: Social Community describe channels of social media focused on *social relationships* and the common activities people participate in with others who share the same interest. Thus, social communities feature two-way and multi-way communication, conversation, collaboration, and the sharing of experiences and resources.

All social media channels are built around networked relationships, but for social communities the interaction and collaboration for relationship building and maintenance are the primary reason people engage in these activities. Many of the channels in which people already participate are placed in this first zone.

The channels in the social community zone include social networking sites, message boards and forums, and wikis. All of them emphasize individual contributions in the context of a community, communication and conversation, and collaboration.

The most used social media vehicles in this zone are Facebook, Twitter, LinkedIn and Google.

Figure 4.1: The four zones of Social Media

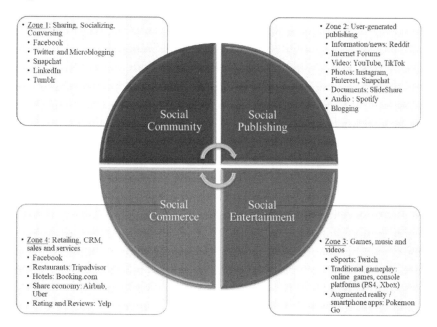

Source: Based on Tuten and Solomon (2015), Figure 1.2 and 1.3, modified

4.2.1 Facebook

Facebook is an American company and online social media and social net-working service based in California. The Facebook website was launched on in February, 2004, by Mark Zuckerberg, along with fellow Harvard College students and roommates. Facebook, Inc. held its initial public offering (IPO) in February 2012, and reached an original peak market capitalization of $104 billion after three months on the stock market. On July 13, 2015, Facebook became the fastest company in the Standard & Poor's 500 Index to reach a market cap of $250 billion. As of January 2017, Facebook was the most popular social networking site in the world, based on the number of active user accounts.

In 2019, Facebook achieved a turnover of 70.7 billion US dollars. Most of Facebook's revenue comes from advertising Facebook generally has a lower click-through rate (CTR) for advertisements than most major websites. The cause of Facebook's low CTR has been attributed to especially younger users enabling ad blocking software and their ability to ignore advertising messages, as well as the site's primary purpose being social communication rather than content viewing. Facebook is the social media giant and as such businesses cannot overlook this global communication channel. Thus, developing a business presence on Facebook is a must, but this is far from simple. First, many people view Facebook primarily for communicating with family and close friends. This means that business connections, advertisements, and intrusive messages may not always be welcome. Consequently, businesses need to carefully plan their interactions in ways that respect typical Facebook use. This is not to say all people prefer to avoid any commercial contact on Facebook at all. In fact, on any given day, millions of Likes are given to corporate pages and business content is viewed, downloaded, and commented upon.

Pages, Profiles and Groups

The fine line between business and personal use is reflected in Facebook's organizational structure in the form of **profiles**, **pages** and **groups**. These structures are intended to give different levels of interaction and have been used to varying degrees by businesses and individuals.

Profiles are the basic structure in Facebook and are intended for individual use (Figure 4.2).

Another feature on Facebook is **groups**. Groups are meant to allow a subset of people to interact and share information. Groups are a private space that can be configured in different ways. Groups can be private so only members can see it, know who is in it and what other members post. A secret group could be used for company employees or a set of business associates (Bulygo, 2010).

Closed groups, on the other hand, can be seen by everyone and everyone will be able to see the membership list. However, the content is only open to members.

Finally, open groups can be seen by anyone, membership is open and all content can be seen by the public. Groups are intended for use with profiles but can be used in some business settings.

Figure 4.2: Individual profile of Philip Kotler

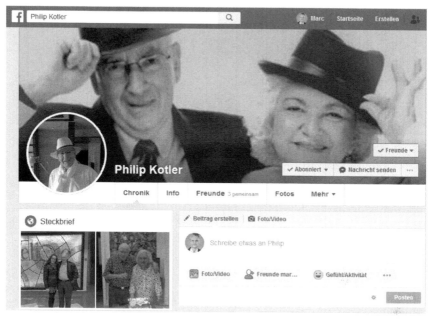

Source: https://www.facebook.com/philip.kotler.39; accessed 15th April 2020

Facebook **pages**, on the other hand, are specifically designed for business use. These do have many of the same features as a user's profile. Users can connect with a page and become a fan of it. Pages can have public messaging walls, events, photos, and custom applications (Figure 4.3).

One of the most useful aspects of Facebook is the ability for people to 'like' and 'tag' the things you do on the site. When users like your page or something you posted on it by pressing the little thumbs-up 'Like' button, the fact that they like it will eventually on their Facebook profiles for their friends to see.

Figure 4.3: Facebook page of Marc Oliver Opresnik

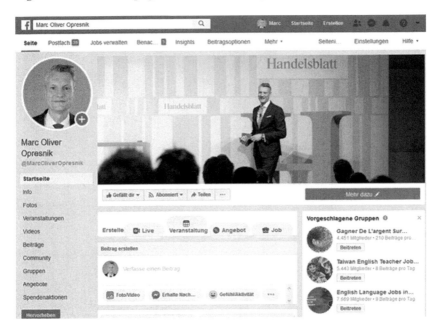

Source: https://www.facebook.com/MarcOliverOpresnik/; accessed 4th May 2020

The same thing is true when you tag something, which is when you identify people within a post or a photo on Facebook. When you tag people, they automatically get notifications that point them to the tagged content.

However, as with other forms of web content, you should always bear in mind not to use social media platforms to overtly sell. Instead, create information that people will want to share as it adds value (Bulygo, 2010).

How to Set Up a Business Page

Business pages are valuable for many reasons, the most obvious being that more than a billion people use Facebook and it is important to meet customers where they congregate. Users become fans of a business page simply by clicking a 'Like' button. This creates a like between their profile and the business page if they are logged into Facebook. Each time a person presses the 'Like' button, the business icon will be placed onto the user's profile page. This provides visibility for the enterprise and helps information to move through networks of friends. Smith (Smith, 2010) provides information regarding the development of a Facebook page for business use. At the beginning, it is advisable to study other Facebook pages to get a sense of what users currently expect. Facebook's directory of pages can be a good starting point to do so (Figure 4.4).

Figure 4.4: Facebook's Directory of Pages

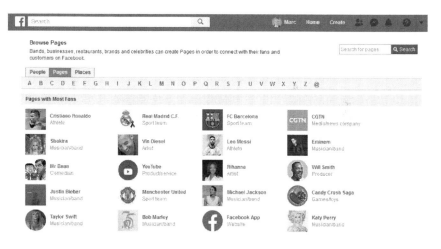

Source: https://www.facebook.com/directory/pages/; accessed 4th May 2020

Smith then recommends a six-step approach to building a business Facebook page. The first step is to determine the page objective. By definition, a page is a single unit of information and not an entire website. This means a primary purpose is paramount. The objective might be leveraging the brand awareness, developing a contact list, driving traffic to a corporate website, developing a sense of community, or gathering ideas for new products. The second step is to devise a design an appropriate strategy. By understanding what needs to be accomplished, decisions regarding the type of media, posts, and other material can be determined. For instance, if the objective was to develop a sense of community, then infrastructure for posting questions and polls can be given a prominent location to support develop a sense of an ongoing conversation with fans (Smith, 2010). Next, a content strategy should be determined. This means deciding whether photos, videos, posts, updates, events, and links should be used and in what kind of mix. Connections to favorite blogs can be supplied in line with custom developed material. The fourth step is to promote the new Facebook page both inside and outside of Facebook. Facebook promotion can be done using a variety of methods: Widgets can be added to Websites, Facebook ads can be placed, blog entries can be written and links back to the page incorporated. In addition, Twitter and print media can be used to drive traffic to the page. Following promotion, engagement and retention are instrumental. Organizational resources will be required to enable the page to be monitored and moderated. Additional page administrators may be required depending on how much traffic is generated. Depending on the page objectives, it may be key to have immediate responses to customer posts or questions. Other forms of engagement might include regular posts, polls, personalized messages to fans and the addition of a discussion board. Finally, the sixth step is to begin converting fans into long-term, loyal customers. Practitioners recommend to wait until the fan base is approximately 500– 1,000 strong. This will enable efforts to achieve measurable results. Conversion can be tricky but it generally involves providing coupons, discounts, special events, or other incentives to give fans a call to action (Smith, 2010).

Facebook pages are the simplest, easiest way to get started marketing with Facebook. They are free, relatively easy to set up (at least in their basic forms), and very flexible.

There is not much of a downside, either. Unfortunately, many companies do not use them to their full potential; or even worse, they use them badly.

The following tips will help you avoid making those mistakes (Bulygo, 2010):

- **Profile Photo and Cover Image:** Your profile photo should ideally be your logo. The cover image is a different story. It is up to you to decide what to put here. Some use photos of employees, while others use fancy artwork and put their contact information in the cover image. Pick a photo that will enhance your page and draw the eye of your visitors.

- **Info/About Section:** The 'About' section is prominently placed right below your company logo. This is your chance to tell anyone coming to your page what your business does. Make sure you put clear information here, telling people what your company does, why you are different, and other appealing details. If you can, take the time to write it specifically for your Facebook audience. Always remember to keep it friendly and informal as a casual tone usually works best on Facebook.

- **Post powerful information:** What you post to your wall will show up in the news feeds of everyone who has 'Liked' your page, just as it does when you post something to your personal profile. For this reason, make sure that what you are posting is useful to your fans. Do not post endless updates about the same thing, and do not post too many updates, clogging the news feeds of your fans. Here are some ideas for the kinds of things you might want to post to your wall:
  - Links to articles related to your company or your industry
  - Links to your blog posts
  - Coupon codes for fans to save on your products
  - New product announcements
  - Links to online tools your fans might find useful

- **Ask Your Fans Questions**: Getting your fans involved with your page is a great way to inspire and enhance loyalty. Asking questions in your updates gets people engaged and involved, but on their own terms. What you ask depends largely on your product and your niche, but asking open-ended questions usually gets you the best responses. Asking opinions on a new product idea can be a good way to convince your fans that your company cares about what they want. If you outperform others in this respect, you may even reach the top of the Facebook News Feed.

- **Do not Spam**: Spam is one of the quickest ways to lose fans. If you do nothing but send out predominantly promotional information about your company and your products, without ever adding anything of value, then you are going to have a hard time getting and keeping fans. Before you send out any update, ask yourself if it honestly adds value to the conversation. If not, do not send it.

- **Study Your Statistics and Results**: Facebook offers useful analytics for pages. Pay attention to them. If you see a big surge in fans (or a drop off), look at what you have posted recently and see if you can figure out a reason for the trend. Consequently, post more of that kind of content (or less, if you're losing fans).

- **Run competitions**: Some of the most successful marketing campaigns done by Facebook pages are via contests. If Facebook competitions are run correctly with good applications & are sufficiently promoted, they can be extremely useful for your Facebook page.

- **Be human**: In addition to putting a face/name to your social media presence, your page also needs to respond like a human by taking into consideration the following aspects:
  - Reply to comments using the person's first name
  - Show Empathy
  - Treat people with Respect

How to Encourage the Development of a Community

Businesses should use their pages to develop a rapport with customers by regularly issuing posts to help foster relationships and to stimulate an active online community. A consistent voice and authentic, original information can encourage people to interact with the business.

We suggest the following items to encourage the development of a community (Kawasaki and Fitzpatrick, 2014):

- **New Content:** Photos, videos, menus, sneak peeks, new product information and event announcements.

- **Questions:** Stimulate customers to provide feedback and opinions about products and services.
- **Events:** Information about new product launches, anniversaries, promotions, in-store events and sales.
- **Stories:** Posts that provide stories about products, successes, or other customers.
- **Embed videos:** Videos are a good way to add to the attractiveness and appeal of your Facebook page.

How to Increase Engagements with Groups and Apps

A great way for organizations of all kinds to keep interested stakeholders informed is to gather them into a Facebook **group**. All users can create groups, and their membership can be closed (by invitation only) or open (anyone can join). Facebook groups are typically for more in-depth communications around a specific subject, while Facebook pages are typically for more loose and more generic communication.

Setting up a Facebook group is very straightforward and it takes just a few minutes. The process includes a built-in tool for sending invitations to your Facebook friends. You should also mention the group on your organization's regular website or blog.

People join Facebook groups because they want to stay informed, and they want to do it on their own time. Just as with blogs, the best way to maintain a group is simply to make valuable information available.

Another great way to build your brand on Facebook is the ability to make **applications**. As an open platform, Facebook allows anybody to create applications that allow friends to share information on the service in different ways. One example is the application 'The Cities I've visited' from TripAdvisor. It displays a map on a user's private Facebook page where virtual thumbtacks can be placed in the cities which have been visited. This is an entertaining and personal way of keeping track of personal travelling. TripAdvisor's business is providing unbiased hotel reviews, photos, and travel advice, so the application is a powerful marketing tool for the company.

Facebook applications are a powerful way for marketers to be creative and try something new, and there is always the possibility for an application to catch fire and go viral.

Facebook's page insights provides statistics to help you determine what is working for your account. You should use this data for targeting your sponsored posts, finding out what posts are popular, and understanding the demographics of your fans (Kawasaki and Fitzpatrick, 2014).

Setting a Business Policy for Facebook

Using Facebook for business, even a small organization, requires functional organization and a consistent approach. For this reason, it becomes important to assign the responsibility for Facebook or any other social media updates to the correct entity within a company. Many businesses assigned social media and website responsibility to an IT department or a technology person. However, effective use requires content development and expertise from functional business areas that communicate with targeted stakeholders. This implies that social media used to communicate with those outside an organization is best served by a media specialist or someone from a marketing or customer service background. Internal use of social media may come from human resources or various departmental managers. While IT people are key members of a social media team, they are rarely the correct people to develop and post content and respond to comments.

A good approach is to set up a **social media team** and use that entity to manage content, updates, approaches, and provide a general strategy. A team might comprise functional managers, media specialists, marketing specialists, copy writers, and technology people. Ultimately, one particular person should oversee the effort. Social media posts or content should be subject to an editorial process and comply with a set of editorial guidelines. It is important to have guidelines defining comments as spam if they include links to non-related content or if the posted comment is self-promoting. A policy might be to ensure every comment receives a thoughtful and adequate response. Another policy might be to ensure posts appear regularly and that post contains original content from within the organization. You might consider to ask thought provoking questions to get customer input or feedback. Perhaps new product development ideas can use Facebook communication to determine customer needs. The potential depends on organizational goals and the resources available to your organization (Kawasaki and Fitzpatrick, 2014).

Facebook provides the ability to manage a company page from an administrative panel. This means the business owner can track activity, respond to comments, and track page statistics. Consequently, a business can learn the identity of its page visitors, the day of week most visitors come to the page, the frequency of comments and which posts generate the most interest. Unlike individual profiles, pages do not accumulate friends. Instead, people become fans of the respective page. Pages provide additional benefits. For instance, users do not have to be logged into Facebook to view a business page. They do not even need a Facebook account. Each page is indexed by Google and other search engines and will be listed when searches are conducted. From a business perspective, pages can be promoted with sidebar ads on Facebook, customized tabs with coupons and other items (e.g. maps, videos, et cetera), or discussions with fans.

Targeted Advertising

Because it gathers so much demographic information about its users, Facebook is one of the best platforms for targeted advertising. You can target users based on practically anything you might find in their profiles, as well as track your success with each segment. Ads can be run on a per-click or per-impression basis. Facebook shows you what bids are for ads like yours, so you know if your bid is in line with others in your industry. You also can set daily limits so there's no risk of blowing your budget (Bulygo, 2010).

There are several different ad types you can choose from: You can create ads that direct to your Facebook page, or to a site not on Facebook. You can also create ads to promote a Facebook event or you can create ads for mobile app installs and app engagement. As stated, you can target by virtually anything on a user's profile, for instance the location, if that is important. You can specify either city, zip code, county, or state. This works particularly well for small and medium sized as well as for local businesses.

From there, you can choose basic demographics, including relationship status, age, workplace, education (including major and years of attendance), birthday, and much more. You can also target ads to people who have recently moved. So, if you own a gym in Hamburg and want to find all the individuals who recently moved to the area, you can target your ads and ad copy to those individuals. Apart from that, you may also target people based on their interests. If, for example, you have a product that is targeted at baseball fans, you could enter baseball in the interest's field. Or, maybe you have recently published a book and you are certain that people who like another certain book will like yours. In that case, you can enter the book's title under interests, and you will specifically target those users. You even can target a private list of users. If you have a list of email addresses of people that you want to target, you can use Facebook's ads manager to target just those people. So, if you run a SAP consulting business and have 300 people on your 'prospect list,' you can use their email addresses to target them with ads in Facebook (Bulygo, 2010).

The other great advantage to tightly-targeted ads is that you can create different ads for different demographic groups. Better-targeted ads are going to lead to better results. If you are targeting baseball fans, you might create individual ads for different popular teams. You could have one ad specifically aimed at Red Sox fans, one at Yankees fans, and another at Cubs fans, and then have those ads shown only to people who have indicated in their interests that they are fans of those specific teams.

Exhibit 4.1

Oreo as a best practice example for sophisticated Facebook marketing

Oreo continues to set the standards for effective Facebook marketing with their beloved cookie. The company utilizes appealing images combined with recipes.

Figure 4.5: Appealing images at Oreo's Facebook site to promote the value proposition

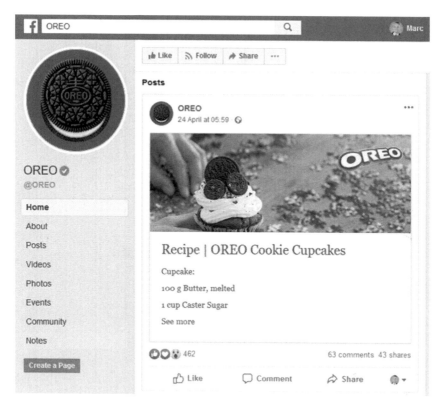

Source: https://www.facebook.com/oreo/; accessed 4th May 2020

In addition, the well-known cookie brand successfully utilizes video ad campaigns to talk to their consumers and also in the framework of new product launches. In a meanwhile classic campaign, Oreo had launched Oreo Mini in Vietnam in 2018, aiming at a wider audience to expand its reach beyond urban centers. The brand recut existing TV commercials to create a series of mobile-optimized videos and animations. Important branding and messaging were shown in the first few seconds, as well as text overlays for sound-off environments. The campaign also ran both video and photo ads in carousel format and also involved reach and frequency buying to find a wider audience and connect with people enough times to make an impact in several key cities across Vietnam. Oreo paired this with automatic placements to ensure optimized ad delivery across the Facebook family of apps.

Over a 4-week period in April–May 2018, the campaign reached over 11 million people in 4 weeks and lifted the brand awareness significantly.

Facebook Watch, a new platform for shows on Facebook to challenge YouTube & Co.

On 9th August 2017, Facebook announced a new video platform called 'Watch' which features live and recorded show episodes. Facebook has been trying for years to become a major player in digital video, but still lags behind its competitors such as Netflix, Amazon Prime Video or YouTube. The service features some live events that Facebook has acquired streaming rights for, including a weekly Major League Baseball game.

Other shows will be produced by video partners including NASA, National Geographic and the NBA. Partners who produce original video content exclusively for Facebook will earn 55% of revenue generated by ad breaks inserted into the content, leaving Facebook with the remaining share. Viewers will be able to personalize their feeds and follow shows and videos they like, much like YouTube's channel subscription model. They will also be able to comment in real time, and a tab will show them what their friends are watching.

With this strategy, Facebook has revamped its video offering, creating a new, TV-like rival to YouTube in order to get people to spend even more time on the social network - time that can be used to show them more ads, generating another option for companies to place products and services therein and also increase the social network's revenue.

Watch replaces the Videos tab within the Facebook mobile app, which launched in 2016. It will also be available on desktop and via Facebook's TV apps, including those made for Apple TV and Amazon Fire TV. Instead of just providing a stream of video content, as the Videos tab used to do, Facebook Watch organizes content into sections like 'most talked about' or 'what's making people laugh'.

The focus on community ties into Facebook's revamped 2017 mission to give people the power to build community and bring the world closer together (Solon, 2017).

4.2.2 Twitter and Microblogging

Microblogging is a special form of blogging which limits the size of each post. The most important microblogging platform is **Twitter**. Twitter Inc. is based in San Francisco and has more than 25 offices around the world. It was created in March 2006 by Jack Dorsey, Noah Glass, Biz Stone, and Evan Williams and launched in July, whereby the service rapidly gained worldwide popularity. Twitter is primarily a social networking service where users post and interact with messages, so-called "tweets", limited to 280 characters (the company regularly raised the upper limit from 140 to 280 text characters in November 2017). Registered users can post tweets, but those who are not registered can only read them. In 2017, Twitter reached $731.6 million in revenue, its first ever profit. In 2019, the company reached $3.46 billion in revenue.

For most companies, it is instrumental to be on Twitter: It is easy, requires very little investment of time, and can quickly prove valuable in increased buzz, turnover and customer insight. Corporations may use Twitter to announce special offers or events, promote new blog posts, or keep followers in the know with links to important news stories. However, growing a real following on Twitter takes more than sending out Tweets whenever the company has a product being released or an upcoming event. It is more about connecting with the target audience and interacting with them.

The following paragraphs will generically introduce the basic elements of microblogging with a special reference being given to Twitter as the current dominant platform in this respect.

Account

On Twitter, individual and company accounts exist alongside a wide range of fictional and inanimate accounts. Many successful people use their first and last names joined together into one long string as their username. You can use your company or business name as your username, and you can fill in that business name in the name text box on the settings page for your account. But if you do, be sure to include the names of anyone who handles the company Twitter account in the 160-character 'bio' text box on the settings page for your Twitter profile (Zarella, 2010). Be aware that your Twitter name has power and influence on **search engine optimization (SEO)**, which translates to how close to the top of a search results list you appear in a search engine such as Yahoo! or Google. If you're a business, consider using a valuable keyword as your Twitter name. Here are a more few tips to keep in mind when choosing a Twitter username (Zarella, 2010; Kawasaki and Fitzpatrick, 2014):

- A good username is the same, or like, your own name. If users have already claimed those names, try adding an adjective or descriptor, such as @philkotler. If you prefer for people not to know who you are, you can choose a name that's a bit more generic.
- You also can use a handle that you've established on other websites. For example, you may want your username to match your e-mail address; if your e-mail address is peter1980@whatever.com, you may decide to use @peter1980 as your Twitter name.
- If you choose to use only your last name as a username, you may find yourself without a first name in the eyes of other Twitterers.
- If you'd prefer to use a nickname rather than your name, or your company or product name, be sure to choose a username that's friendly and accessible.
- Use a rather short Twitter username. Tweets are only 280 characters, so when people are replying to you, and in case you have a longer name, you leave them less room for message content. Twitter limits your username to just 15 characters for this very reason.

Avatar

Your Twitter account requests 2 photos, your header photo, which appears on your profile page, and your profile photo, which appears on every one of your tweets. This image is also called your Twitter avatar. When people read your tweets, they will be shown next to a small image you have uploaded to Twitter. This picture is how most people will recognize tweets as being yours, so use something that stands out and do not change it frequently. For personal accounts, a good-quality portrait is the best option, for company accounts, your logo will work, if it is recognizable in a small size. A good avatar does two things. First it validates who you are by providing picture. Second, it supports the narrative that you are likeable, trustworthy, and competent (Zarella, 2010).

Here are a few more basics to keep in mind when choosing a Twitter avatar (Zarella, 2010; Kawasaki and Fitzpatrick, 2014):

- The photo must be clear, crisp and use the small space as best it can. That means that using a photo where you're in the middle of a crowd is not a good idea.
- While changing your avatar is easy, stay consistent. Let your followers see a consistent image of a span of time – it builds your brand.
- Consider conveying a short message serving as a tagline. Make this a mantra – two or four words that explain why you or your organization exists.
- Face the light. The source of light should come from in front of you.
- Think big. When people scan posts and comments, the see your avatar at a postage-stamp size. When they click on it, however, they should see a big, crisp photo, so upload a picture with an adequate number of pixels.

Background

Twitter gives you the ability to design and upload a custom background image for your account page. Some users and companies add lots of extra information, including other social sites where they can be found. This is not advisable as people who read your tweets can be distracted by what else you've got going on the screen. The best custom background image to use is one that shows your company's colors or logo to reinforce your brand image (Zarella, 2010).

Figure 4.6: Twitter page of Porsche

Source: https://twitter.com/Porsche/; accessed 4th May 2020

Like your websites and blogs, your Twitter page should reflect your business or your personality. And that means paying attention to the background. Just be sure to follow these rules (Kawasaki and Fitzpatrick, 2014):

- Use something relevant and representative to what you do.
- Think about potential customers. Will they want to see this?

CV and Bio

When you are creating your account, you will have 160 characters in a comprised bio section to explain who you are. This takes very little time to write and practical experience shows, that accounts with bios have far more followers on average than accounts without bios.

Followers

When you follow someone on Twitter, you will see the respective tweets in the timeline of that person and vice versa. The number of followers you have is the number of people who will potentially be exposed to your tweets, so to increase your reach and impact, you should try to get more followers (Zarella, 2010).

Tweets

The core of Twitter is, of course, the tweet: a 280-character or less text message posted. These messages can be seen by anyone with an Internet connection or mobile device and are stored sequentially on webpages that can be searched and reviewed. The messages are intended to share and spread information with anyone who follows the account but can be accessed through public searches and other ways. Every tweet from all a user's subscribed accounts is stored in a so-called timeline. Collectively, this creates a huge information network storing millions of messages available for research and business intelligence applications.

Businesses use Twitter for different purposes, ranging from marketing to customer service to product development. Twitter can be particularly powerful for new companies and small and medium sized enterprises and can result in the quick and wide spread of information. As a graphic is worth a thousand words do ensure to make use of it by including pictures in your tweets.

Bear in mind, however, that Twitter is not merely a tool to drive traffic to the company website. If you want to successfully use this powerful tool think of using Twitter to create a dialog and gather business information. In addition, be sure to assign the correct Tweeters. These people need to be knowledgeable, good listeners and trustworthy as they will represent a company to the world. Remember that all tweets are public and once they have been sent out, it is nearly impossible to effectively retract what has been stated. Ensure you follow the right people and subscribe to high quality Twitter feeds (Zarella, 2010).

Replies

When you start a tweet with an @username, only people who are following both you and @username will see your tweet. If you want more people to see it, just put a period or other marker in front of the username. Or you can always just rephrase your sentence. Likewise, you can see who has mentioned your name by clicking on the '@username' link when you are logged in to Twitter. Replies such as this are still public if someone views your account or uses the sear function. To be approachable and genuinely interested in dialogues, you should respond to as many messages as you can (Kawasaki and Fitzpatrick, 2014).

Retweets

Retweets are the most powerful mechanisms for marketers on this platform. If a company tweets something, its followers ill see it. If they retweet it, a message can spread virally through Twitter, reaching tens or hundreds of times as many people as it would if only a single person tweeted it. In this respect, it can be helpful to as your followers to retweet something you have posted.

Here are a few points to get you started (Zarella, 2010; Kawasaki and Fitzpatrick, 2014):

- Try to credit at least the original user who posted the tweet.
- If the original tweet included a call to action (such as 'please retweet'), try to keep that in your retweet.
- If the original tweet has a link, keep it in there.
- Try to keep as much of the original tweet intact as possible.

Direct Messages

Direct messages (DMs) are the private messages of Twitter. DMs are great when you need private information, like an address. Traditionally, you can only send DMs to people who follow you and vice versa. If you have a verified account through Twitter, you can select a special setting to allow anyone to send you DMs. However, you cannot respond via DMs unless the respective person follows you. Please bear in mind never to send automated DMs as it is considered spam. In addition, do not send auto-DMs to your followers as these are not engaging, and you are not reaching out personally for relationship building. If you would like to reach out to every single person that decides to follow you, do so in a personalized and unique way although this is more time-consuming (Zarella, 2010; Kawasaki and Fitzpatrick, 2014).

Trending Topics

Twitter has developed an algorithm that tracks mentions of words and phrases up to three words long, and highlight those that are the most talked about at any given point of time. You will find this as a top 10 list in the right-hand column of your Twitter page. If your company's name appears in this list, it can drive significant amount of buzz and awareness. The trending topics section is a good barometer for what the Twitter community is currently interested in and talking about (Zarella, 2010).

Twitter and Marketing Research

Every marketing and PR person should monitor what people are saying about their organization, their products and services, and perhaps their competitors. If you have never done this, please do it right now, because it can be an eye-opening experience to see what people are saying. A great way to use Twitter and other social media platforms to monitor what people are saying is to use a Twitter **client application** such as TweetDeck or Hootsuite. These applications allow you to monitor multiple keywords and phrases in real time so you know instantly when something important is mentioned.

Hashtags

To connect ideas and conversation topics into a cohesive stream, people often use hashtags. Simply a word preceded by the pound or number sign '#', a hashtag, is used to indicate that a certain tweet is about the same topic as every other tweet using the same name tag. By using hashtags, you are exposing yourself to a wider audience. Many people follow conversations using various hashtags, but possibly will not be following you. Hashtags are meant as a shortcut to explain what your tweet contains or to show you are part of a conversation or event. If your brand is jumping into a hashtag, you should make sure that you're contributing value to the conversation instead of just promoting your business. If you want to utilize hashtags do pick a short, unique one which is easy to remember and leaves enough character for retweets. Such a hashtag increases brand awareness once the chat is over and is useful if your chat becomes a regular event. You do not want to have to retrain people to use a new hashtag. An example can be your brand such as #Nike (Kawasaki and Fitzpatrick, 2014)..

Shortened URLs

Since each tweet has a 280-character limit, space is precious. URLs tend to be rather long and take up too much space in a tweet, so a handful of services have been developed that allow you to shorten links. With these services, you enter a URL, and then the service returns a much shorter version which redirects visitors to the correct address. Although Twitter now auto-shortens your links, you should consider using a separate shortening service with built-in analytics, as it will allow you to track clicks of your content that do not point back to your own web properties (Zarella, 2010; Kawasaki and Fitzpatrick, 2014).

Responsiveness

Due to the condensed format and rapid pace of Twitter, it is essential to respond to your community as swiftly as possible. The platform makes it easy for people to find your brand, and you are sure to get many customer service requests that need your immediate attention. If you ignore a critical tweet for too long, you may find that one person's voice is soon amplified by their followers. Additionally, do not just respond to emergencies or questions—make sure you also say hello and respond to kudos given to your brand. As you grow, you will have to figure out how scale, but too much tweeting is a great problem to have (Kawasaki and Fitzpatrick, 2014).

Exhibit 4.2

Innocent as a best practice example for effective Twitter marketing

While Innocent may be a smoothie and juice brand, they stay far away from pushily promoting their products.

Figure 4.7: Typical humorous tweet by Innocent

In fact, most of their social media posts are not about smoothies or drinks at all. Instead, they use social media to foster their silly, fun, clever, and creative brand personality.

They simply want to talk to people and inform them about the company in the most engaging way.

The goal is to make its page a place on social media which people want to visit and enjoy seeing in their time-lines.

Consequently, people will not mind when the company tries to sell them drinks every now and again.

Figure 4.8: Non-product related tweet by Innocent

Source: https://twitter.com/innocent; accessed 4th May 2020

It is this content marketing approach to Twitter that makes Innocent stand out from the crowd -- and it certainly works for their audience.

How to Use Twitter as a Marketer

When you are ready to set up your own Twitter profile and begin to tweet, the most important aspect from the marketing perspective is to not use this service – and neither any other social media platform – as an advertising channel to take up your products and services. As a way to think about your social media activities, we would suggest to follow 'The Sharing More Than Selling Rule' which states that you should be doing 85 per cent sharing and engaging, 10 per cent publishing original content, and only 5 per cent or even less promoting what you are trying to sell. Sharing and engaging included things as commenting on someone else's blog or Facebook post, quoting a tweet and adding your take, or responding to somebody who has said something interesting. Most people, especially those new to a social network, do not share end engage enough. Since sharing and engaging is the easiest aspect of social networking, it should not take much for you to do more of it. Next to sharing and engaging, it is instrumental to have about 10 per cent of your social interactions be publishing something original. You can share a photo, write a blog post, compose a tweet about something that interests your marketplace, or publish a video. The more helpful this content is to your buyer personas the better. Finally, only 5 per cent of your social interactions should involve something that you want to promote to your audience. This is when you share a new product your company offers, a special discount for social followers, or other content of a promotional nature. Most companies and people sell way too much and as such their social feeds do not have much interaction. People just do not want to be sold to. However, if you are helpful and engaging and responsive on your social feeds, then you build an audience who will want to hear from you and who will be receptive to learning about what you and your organization does (Scott, 2015).

4.2.3 LinkedIn

LinkedIn was founded in 2002 and it is based in California, USA. The company was acquired by Microsoft in December 2016 for $26.2 billion. LinkedIn is mainly used for professional networking, including employers posting jobs and job seekers posting their CVs. As of 2015, most of the site's revenue came from selling access to information about its users to recruiters and sales professionals. LinkedIn derives its revenues from three business units:

- **Talent Solutions,** through which recruiters and corporations pay for branded corporation and career listing pages, pay-per-click targeted job ads, and access to the LinkedIn database of users.
- **Marketing Solutions,** which advertisers pay for pay per click-through targeted ads.
- **Premium Subscriptions,** through which LinkedIn users can pay for advanced services, such as LinkedIn Business, LinkedIn Talent (for recruiters), LinkedIn Job Seeker, and LinkedIn Sales for sales professions.

LinkedIn is a powerful platform for growing the reach of a company's business and attracting new clients or customers. The key to this is the use of segmentation by job-functions, geography and other criteria. By segmentation it is possible to reach a more specific target group of key decision makers (for buying specific products/services) within specific industries. LinkedIn also presents an opportunity to stay top of mind with employees, customers, vendors, partners and industry influencers if it is possible to publish relevant content to these key stakeholders (Zarella, 2010).

In terms of customization and integration, LinkedIn is the most restrictive social network. It does not, for example, include any photo-sharing features, and was the last of the major social networks to allow users to post photos of themselves to their profiles. The key function is professional networking, so LinkedIn is primarily used by job seekers and recruiters. The platform restricts contact between members so that only users who are directly contacted can message each other. While Facebook focuses on connections between friends, relatives, and other casual acquaintances, LinkedIn has specifically courted the business world and attempted to create an online venue where job histories, resumes, recommendations, and career-related networking can occur. Many businesses recruit new employees using the platform and for many individuals, LinkedIn has become the prime location where all business contacts, skill inventories, training records, and experience histories are maintained. LinkedIn is also useful in maintaining communication and contact with business associates. For instance, if a member changes jobs, locations, or receives a promotion, the updated information can be shared easily and spread among the respective business associates (Zarella, 2010).

Profiles on LinkedIn

Much like Facebook, LinkedIn relies on profiles for individual users. The primary difference relates to the type of material that is important to LinkedIn users. The primary profile components for LinkedIn are as follows:

- **Picture:** This is a unique photo of the profile owner. Most users prefer pictures showing that individual wearing business attire.
- **Positions:** This is a list of current and past job positions including dates, titles, job duties, responsibilities, and other pertinent information.
- **Achievements:** A profile holder can provide a summary of his or her primary achievements.
- **Education History:** This is a list of all education and training attended. Generally, it focuses on university experience and degrees but can include other training venues as well.
- **Links:** A list of links can be added. Most users include links to their blogs, company website, or other important locations relevant to work life.

In principal, LinkedIn includes a basic resume, a personal summary, contact details, and links to pertinent websites. All of those are focused on professional networking. Like mentioned above, LinkedIn offers different levels of access. By upgrading to a paid premium account, additional capabilities are added. Among these are faster searches of LinkedIn's membership database, direct messaging without needing introductions, and more profile organization tools and options (Zarella, 2010).

Once a profile has been created, a LinkedIn user can publish it and begin establishing connections. Connections are current and former colleagues, classmates, business associates, and other professional contacts. In general, the idea is to create direct connections by adding people relevant to your professional circle. These connections can provide introductions to additional professionals which help build a network in specialty areas. LinkedIn's connections can provide ways to find freelance and consulting work as well. It is possible to include information to aid others seeking business consultants. In addition, it is also possible to use connections to build business customer bases, seek new sales leads, or to find new career opportunities. Among the featured uses of LinkedIn are the following:

- Obtain, store and share online recommendations that can be used to attest to professional abilities or character.
- Obtain introductions to key individuals in relevant branches.
- Obtain introductions to potential employers.
- Search job listings.
- Create an online resume that continues to grow.

LinkedIn also provides **interest groups** that allow members to engage in threaded discussions. Individuals participating in groups may be invited to join professional networks by others in the conversations. Discussions can be used to post job listings.

LinkedIn also permits resumes to be searched by professionals seeking to recruit top talent into their firms. Groups are a great way to meet people in your industry and discuss career-related topics and subject areas (See Figure 4.9).

You can choose to receive e-mail notifications for conversations that you are taking part in.

Figure 4.9: LinkedIn group 'Marketing & Negotiation Experts Global'

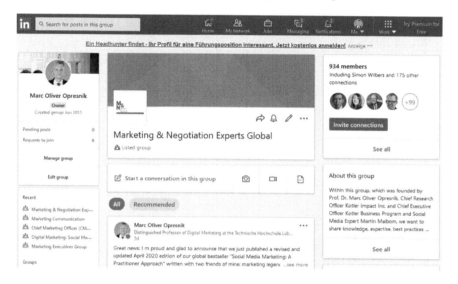

Source: https://bit.ly/3f0bv68; accessed 4th May 2020

LinkedIn Company Pages

The idea of a company page is to allow businesses to post additional details that will be of interest to current or potential employees, stakeholders, and the general public. A company page can provide news feed type features where updates, changes, and news can be posted. Many companies have started to use company pages to create special offers for visitors and those that recommend or endorse the page. Like the company pages found on Facebook, these pages are open to the public and can be found with search engines. It is instrumental for a company to include their contact details, email addresses, and other details on these pages.

Recommendations

An important feature specific to LinkedIn is recommendations. With this feature, users can write short endorsements of other users they have worked with. During a job search, these recommendations can powerfully function as a form of reference (Zarella, 2010).

LinkedIn for Job Searches

LinkedIn is also known for its capability as a job search tool. In many ways, it has disrupted the industry and become the new standard for posting resumes, recommendation letters, and providing career histories. Potential employers can easily see prospective hires' networks of contacts which can add to the applicants' credibility and reputation. Many employers use LinkedIn exclusively for job postings which, of course, emphasizes the importance of having a LinkedIn account and a complete profile.

Using LinkedIn to find a new position means ensuring a profile is set up to emphasize the applicant's strengths. While most jobs still require a separate resume and cover letter, LinkedIn profiles may be used for screening to provide a more comprehensive picture. This means the entire 'resume' portion of the profile should be complete, error-free, updated, and relevant to the type of work being sought after.

Against this background, LinkedIn can also be used to discover and join groups related to the work field desired. This provides more opportunities and demonstrates to potential employers the relevance of the job as well as the commitment of a potential applicant. Once a group member, it becomes possible for a job seeker to invite potential employers to join their network or to participate in direct discussions.

Finding jobs on LinkedIn starts with the 'Jobs' tab. LinkedIn will then generate a list of potentially relevant jobs based on a user's resume and job history by trying to match up key words in job listings (See Figure 4.10). By default, this provides views of jobs that may match potential search criteria. The system also provides advanced search features to allow a user to broaden their search or narrow in on a certain job category.

In general, the serious and professional nature of LinkedIn means that you should not share quotes or popular memes such as cat pictures. You should assume that a potential employer or business partner will check your

LinkedIn posts. Thus, you should seldom share post on LinkedIn containing a YouTube video, for example, simply with the intent of entertaining people. Instead, share your SlideShare presentations and other professional content as a short-form LinkedIn update and embed them in long-term published posts.

In addition, it is advisable to stay focused on a few core topics to establish thought leadership. Philip shares content on Corporate Social Responsibility and innovation. Svend, in particular, is more dedicated to global marketing whereas Marc specializes on marketing and brand communication, in particular social media, and negotiation. All of us share other relevant articles that we like, but our focus is on our niches.

Figure 4.10: LinkedIn job search example

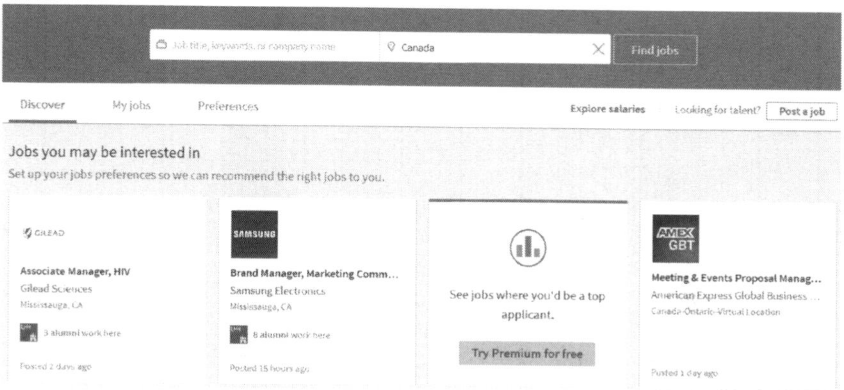

Source: http://bit.ly/29wHb5B; accessed 11th February 2017

Exhibit 4.3

AppleOne as a best practice example for a powerful LinkedIn presence

As an employment agency, AppleOne could simply push their job openings on LinkedIn. Instead, they share value-adding content and advice for job seekers both from their blog and from other outlets.

Figure 4.11: Value-adding content by AppleOne on their LinkedIn page

AppleOne Employment Services The five lies you'll hear when you go in for a job interview. http://bit.ly /2jnRl8b

Like (44) · Comment (1) · Share · 5 days ago

Source: http://bit.ly/2lqGJb7; accessed 11th February 2017

AppleOne's LinkedIn description also includes information that differentiates them from other, similar companies, while touching on their core mission. For example, they write:

'AppleOne Employment Services is unique in that we view the career seeker as a client. Other employment agencies see you as a commodity to be sold, and it shows in the way they treat you. Our services are always free to our associates, and we encourage you to take full advantage of them.'

4.2.4 Snapchat

Snap Inc. was founded in 2011 and is based in Venice, California. Snap Inc. develops a text and photo based messaging application for mobile phones. The company was formerly known as Snapchat, Inc. and changed its name to Snap Inc. in September 2016. By January 2014, the company had refused offers of acquisition, including overtures from Mark Zuckerberg (Facebook) to buy Snapchat and its assets. At its core, Snapchat is used to send photos and videos to friends. Your friends can view snaps (Photos or videos taken with Snapchat) for up to 10 seconds, and then the snaps disappear. You can also capture a photo or brief video with it, then add a caption or doodle or filter/lens over top, and send the finished creation (the snap) to a friend. Alternatively, you can add your snap to your 'story', a 24-hour collection of all your snaps that's broadcasted to the world or just your followers. Snapchat is mostly a hit among teenagers, according to several research firms, though it is catching on and embracing new demographics every day.

Against this background, Snapchat has gone from being a simple photo and video sharing app to a marketing tool that cannot be ignored. The app has come a long way since its beginnings in 2011; self-destructing photos and video are no longer just for smartphone-savvy teens but for marketers who want a creative way to reach their target audience. However, utilizing this platform to effectively connect with a potential customer can be tricky. It is worth noting that Snapchat puts a limit on how long its videos and photos are available for on the app. For instance, a video or photo will disappear as soon as a few seconds go by, never to be seen again by the recipient. This implies that marketers need to make the most of every second they get on the app, which requires a certain amount of strategy.

Understanding Your Target Audience

Even if your target audience are business executives, it is key to grasp the environment of Snapchat. Unlike LinkedIn, Snapchat has always been an app that encourages rather casual communication through the use of videos and photos. People take pictures of their meals, vacations, and daily activities to share with friends – they are not typically displaying professional behavior. Against this background, it is instrumental to emphasize the overall casualness of the app. When your marketing team is creating a strategy specifically for Snapchat, you need to settle on a tone of voice that will be used across the board. Ideally, the language you use should be easy-to-understand, and your posts should have a sense of humor. For instance, you could think about incorporating the drawing function on Snapchat that allows you to add edits to your photos. By doing so your team appears more approachable. If you are just starting out on Snapchat, take some time to browse through other accounts and follow other people to get a better idea of how they use the app (DeMers, 2014).

Capitalize on the Time Limit

While some may perceive the self-destructive nature of Snapchat to be a barrier, you should capitalize on this aspect of the app. More specifically, this feature of the platform gives you an ideal opportunity to offer teasers to your followers. Because videos and photos only exist for a few seconds, you can use Snapchat to give people a preview of an upcoming product or service that your company may be offering. You can also use Snapchat to create **contests**. For example, you can ask other users to send you pictures of them using your product and offer a reward to those who do. The trick to getting the most leverage out of Snapchat is ensuring that you are always looking for ways to engage and communicate with your customers. Doing so can keep people coming back for more, giving you additional opportunities to roll out your marketing strategy more effectively (DeMers, 2014).

Videos do Enhance the Relationship Building Process

Apart from self-destructing photos, videos are a key component of the website as well. Although they also disappear once they have been viewed, marketers can use them to reach out to people who are interested in getting a sneak peek of their office culture, product production, and everything in between (DeMers, 2014).

Exhibit 4.4

General Electric as a best practice example for effectively utilizing Snapchat as a marketing tool in B2B

Would you ever have guessed that General Electric, a multinational conglomerate corporation which is a classic B2B (Business-to-Business) corporation, would have an active and effective presence on Snapchat? In fact, they do (username: @generalelectric) and moreover, they have actually done a great jo of using their platform to showcase their personality and to encourage interest in science -- something the company has done well on other social media networks like Instagram and YouTube.

One of the best ways the company uses the platform is in a series in which they answer users' questions by explaining scientific concepts in a concise and funny way. For example, they recently shared some of their findings from their emoji science curriculum, which they established along with the National Science Foundation.

In addition to sharing their emoji science findings, they also encourage their followers to interact directly with them. 'Just add 'generalelectric' on Snapchat, send us an emoji, and we'll send you some science,' they wrote on their Tumblr account. GE's global director of innovation, Sam Olstein, stated: 'The disappearing nature of its content encourages repeat usage and provides us with a unique way to celebrate invention with an expanding community of young fans.'

Source: Based on Kolowich, L.: 10 of the Best Brands on Twitter, https://blog.hubspot.com/marketing/twitter-best-brands, accessed 11th February 2017

Marketing teams can use video to provide more valuable and engaging content to their followers. Although they say a picture is worth a thousand words, you can verbalize the message you are trying to convey to your audience through a video more effectively.

As it goes with any type of social media, Snapchat provides a powerful way to portray the true intentions and mission of your company, whether it involves providing a service or a valuable product. Ideally, the media that you share over the app should give people a better idea of your business and what you have to offer. You should always be working to inject personality into your photos and videos to help people connect to your brand on a 'human-like' level.

To put it into a nutshell: Use Snapchat to show off more than just content, but what happens behind the scenes. Ask different people at your company to contribute to your Snapchat efforts to add some flavor. If done well, you will notice a difference in how quickly your following grows.

Snapchat Stories

While the basic Snapchat service is interesting as a real-rime communications tool, it has its limitations for classic marketing and public relations communication because of its one-to-one and time limitation. Meanwhile, however, the company has introduced a new feature called 'Snapchat Stories', which is emerging as a new fascinating way to communicate with a market in real time.

A Snapchat story is a photo or video you post to your very own stories section (or feed) of your Snapchat account, which is visible by you and all your friends. To do so, simply swipe from right to left on any tab in the Snapchat app until you see a screen tab labeled 'Stories.' Your friends' stories will appear under 'Recent Updates.' You can tap anybody's name to trigger to view a friend's story, or stories in the order they were posted. Stories live for 24 hours and can be viewed again and again for that period. Once the 24-hour time limit is up, they are automatically deleted. All users can configure their privacy settings so that their stories can be viewed by anyone on Snapchat, just friends or a customized group of users (Siu, 2016).

Snapchat stories allow you to string Snaps together to create a compelling narrative. Snapchat has always been known as a private messaging app, but stories offer a more public way of sharing making it a powerful and innovative tool for marketers. Accordingly, many celebrities, brands and other high profile users share their Snapchat username manually or by snapcode so that any stories they post can be viewed by the thousands and thousands of users who decide to add them. Even though marketers have access to so many other feed-style apps to share our lives with our friends, Snapchat stories are at least a great new option to use if you take a fantastic snap that you would like to be viewable for more than just a few seconds (DeMers, 2014).

Because Snapchat Stories disappear after a day, there is much more of a real-time feel to this service. With apps like Instagram, Twitter and Facebook, your photos and videos live on, so there is little incentive for people to view them right away. Thus, corporations could showcase how their customers use their wares, in particular with highly visual products and services like sporting goods, cars, hotels, restaurants, and the like.

Effective Ways to Use Snapchat as a Marketer

Snapchat can help you build an engaged following, increase loyalty, and boost your brand visibility. In addition to the above-mentioned aspects, here are the most powerful ways to use Snapchat for business (Siu, 2016):

- **Offer exclusive content**: Give your customers a look at what goes on behind the scenes at your company. Global fast-food giant McDonald's (username: mcdonalds) extensively makes use of influencers to promote their products. Professional athletes like LeBron James gave users a behind-the-scenes look at the rollout of the new bacon clubhouse sandwich. Even if your marketing budget is only a fraction of what McDonald's is, customers and other stakeholders still like feeling as if they know the story behind your company.

- **Share Promo Codes**: Frozen yogurt chain 16 Handles (username: love16handles), for example, used Snapchat's instant photo feature to amass followers and promote their frozen treats. They were also among the first brands to use Snapchat for coupon offers. The company managed to earn new customers by promoting specific store locations and times, and when people snapped photos of themselves or their friends eating 16 Handles yogurt, they instantly received a coupon code for between 16% and 100% off. The clue: They only had 10 seconds to show the cashier. You too can get your followers involved with Snapchat-exclusive coupon codes or other exclusive promos. Make it easy and fun to interact with your brand.

- **Allow exclusive access and content**: In the past, it took several weeks for pictures from events such as the 'New York Fashion Week' to trickle down from photographers to magazines, and then from newsstands to consumers. With Snapchat, followers can watch the fashions unfold almost instantly. Several companies make use of this tool and share snaps of models strutting down the catwalk, allowing them to deliver images of the iconic fashion show to people in ways never dreamed of before. As a takeaway, you can use Snapchat to give your followers a VIP look at your events and promotions that they will likely never have a chance to attend in person. This can be a fun, entertaining and easy way to bring new life to established events. So, do consider sharing exclusive information with a limited audience.

- **Demo Your Product and Services**: The world's biggest online retailer, Amazon (username: amazon), used Snapchat to give a personality and voice to Alexa, the company's female-voiced Echo speaker. In a sophisticated use of social media, Amazon employed Snapchat to give clarity to the product as well as to promote Echo. Thanks to its campaign, Amazon gathered 6,100 mentions in just four hours. It demonstrated that Echo was off to a promising start. Against this background, if your brand releases new technology or products, you can use Snapchat as a guide for new customers. It is an innovative and clever way to introduce new products and engage with potential customers.

- **Partner with influencers**: Sour Patch Kids (username: sourpatchsnaps) is a big hit among the Snapchat demographic. Mondelez, the corporation behind the brand, worked with social media personality Logan Paul to produce content for chats. Over the course of just five days, Paul documented childish pranks pulled on unsuspecting people, with the pranks dubbed 'sweet' or 'sour' to highlight the brand's flavors. The brand encouraged fans to post and promote the upcoming story. The campaign earned the company 120,000 new Snapchat followers. Like Sour Patch Kids, you can work with an influencer whose follower base is like yours to share snaps that coincide with your brand's image.

- **Address relevant issues**: Historically, soap brand Dove (username: dove) appealed primarily to older women until it reached out to younger women using Snapchat and other social media platforms. Over a period of two hours, 30 women chatted with psychologists and other ambassadors on the Snapchat platform to share ideas and thoughts about self-esteem issues in a campaign to help boost young women's self-images. The resulting snaps earned the brand 75 conversations and 130,000 views. Takeaway: Do not be afraid to be real. Authenticity is essential on this hyper-social network.

4.2.5 Google Plus+

Google+ (pronounced and sometimes written as Google Plus or just Plus) is an interest-based social network which was founded launched in June 2011 and that is owned and operated by Google. Features included the ability to post photos and status updates to the stream or interest based communities, group different types of relationships into circles, a multi-person instant messaging, text and video chats called Google Hangouts, events, location tagging, and the ability to edit and upload photos to private cloud-based albums.

In addition to being a social network, Plus was meant to be the social layer to all of Google's other products. A user's profile was used for many other services, such as YouTube. The '+1' button was a competitor to Facebook's 'Like' button and was present throughout the web.

Despite the attempts at company-wide integration, Plus never really took off among users at the beginning. The platform was not just regarded as the newcomer, it was often looked down upon as a poser which wants to imitate Facebook.

In November of 2015, Google unveiled a major redesign that put a renewed focus on collections and communities to create an interest-based social network instead.

In January 2017, Google rolled out more updates to the product. The new Plus automatically did hide low-quality comments. Another update entailed zoom capabilities on photos and making it so that you will see less white space on the screen.

On 8 October 2018, Google announced that the data of numerous user had been stolen. At the same time, the company announced that the network is used very little and that 90 percent of all visits do not last longer than five seconds. That's why Google+ was discontinued for private users in April 2019.

On the other hand, companies can still set up and manage brand accounts.

In this way, services such as YouTube can still be used to expand your online presence.

Why a Google Brand Account is Still Important for Businesses

Although Google+ was discontinued for private users, brand accounts will remain important for businesses as they can continue to increase online presence and awareness. The reason for this is that the connection to Google and the strength of its search engine continues to make it important. Because when someone enters your name or company in Google's search engine, the brand profile is one of the best results.

So, if you haven't done it yet, get a brand account and take some time to upload a photo and a description and write some posts (McGorty, 2017; Scott, 2015).

The Best Tips and Tricks for Using Your Brand Account

A brand account can sustainably increase the brand awareness of your company. Here are some tips and tricks to get the most out of your account as a marketer (McGorty, 2017; Scott, 2015; Kawasaki and Fitzpatrick, 2014):

- **Making the Most of your Account**: The very first step to creating a place for your business within the Google world is to create a fully optimized profile page, as described above. This means that all relevant information about your company such as contacts, your logo, a mission statement, products and services, photos and links to your website will be clearly visible. Remember that your brand account is linked to the world's most popular search engine, so everything you share is displayed on the search results page for your business.

- **Capitalize on SEO Opportunities**: It is also recommendable to frequently and strategically insert industry-specific keywords throughout your pages to improve your SEO performance. The Google algorithm prioritizes appropriate pages. Therefore, a high frequency of posts will result in a better overall ranking.

- **Make Use of Google Features**: Today, videos and photos are among the most common forms of content. Google also has a feature called **Google Hangouts** that allows users to record and stream live broadcasts. In addition to presenting an interactive medium between you and your customers, Google Hangouts is ideal for webinars, presentations, workshops, Q&A's, vlogs and announcements. This is a great and cost-effective option for companies that want to produce content that is easily accessible to their target audience. It can also facilitate your company's visibility and presence on the Internet.

- Google also has other features like **Events** that let you create custom invitations for all the events your business hosts.

- **Assess and Encourage Customer Reviews**: Brand sites have a unique opportunity for customers to rate their personal experiences with your company. Although there is no way to filter out the bad reviews from the good ones, both can still be useful for your business.

First of all, pages are integrated with Google search results, so positive reviews will strengthen your authenticity and enhance your customers' trust. Strong reviews will also boost your company's SEO. On the other hand, negative reviews may seem damaging, but they can also be a blessing in disguise as they give you the opportunity to connect with that user and see where it all went wrong. In addition to using any criticism to build on future campaigns, it will show them that your company is dedicated to enhancing customer service and that their voice will always be heard.

4.2.6 Tumblr

Tumblr is a microblogging and social networking website founded by David Karp in 2007, and owned by Yahoo! since 2013. The platform allows users to post multimedia and other content to a short-form blog. Users can follow other users' blogs. As of February 1, 2017, Tumblr hosts over 334.1 million blogs. Tumblr's also accumulating many new users as it continues to grow at a rapid pace, while the platform's active user base publishes over 59 million posts every day. Brands like Calvin Klein, Coca-Cola and adidas are already thriving on the network. However, only a fraction of businesses is taking advantage of the potential Tumblr offers. Thus, this is a great opportunity for you and your business, because when the competition is low, it is easier to standout and build a strong presence (Singca, 2016).

In the following paragraphs, we are exploring some of the best practices that can maximize the efficiency of your Tumblr marketing campaigns (Singca, 2016):

- **Make Sure the Tumblr Audience Matches Your Targeted Demographic**: The first criterion that can help you determine if Tumblr is right for your marketing communication is your audience. Since 3 in 4 Tumblr users are under 35, it's essential to correlate this fact with the demographic you would like to target. Older audiences tend to be more active on Facebook or Twitter, so visual marketing campaigns made for targeting them would make more sense there. Given the age of the audience, it becomes rather clear that the visual content must contain a high dose of humor. In addition, the content should be inspirational. Like with other social media platforms, posting content that is too brand specific and too promotional does not work well.

- **Focus on the Right Type of Content**: Tumblr supports a wide range of content types. You can always change between text, audio, quotes, links, and chats, but the focus is on photos. Considering the network's appeal for this type of content, your marketing team should be able to create a lot of visuals. On June 21, 2016, Tumblr announced that it would also support live video. As live video, can substantially increase the audience's engagement with your brand, it is advisable to make use of this feature. Although Tumblr chose to integrate existing live video solutions (e.g. YouTube, YouNow, Kanvas and Upclose) into its platform, rather than investing in a proprietary live-streaming platform, the platform should not be neglected, as relying on it could help reaching a wider audience.

- **Equip Your Brand's Profile with Everything Needed**: The 'About' page is the first one you should set up after installing a specific theme. This should include a detailed introduction to your company, as well as a link to your website. Also, provide links to other social media profiles to make sure that your profile's visitors get a clearer image of your brand. Reposting content from other platforms is a mistake brands should learn to avoid. Tumblr is a platform with a lot of potential on its own so auto-posting updates from other websites offers users no real benefit.

- **Interact with Your Audience**: As on all other social media networks, engagement is an important performance metric on Tumblr. To start, you might have to begin interacting with your audience first. Liking, reblogging and commenting on other users' updates will get your brand noticed and increase chances they will return the favor.

The above actions should take place after posting several updates on your page. This helps ensure that the people whose posts you have liked or commented on have something to like back. It is instrumental at this point to post images that are representative to your brand. As a next step, you can proceed to reblogging posts that are relevant to your brand. By doing this, you add content to your page and give the original creators more visibility. Liking and commenting are done as on other networks such as Facebook or Pinterest. To increase the chances of engagement, comments should be meaningful and value-adding. Another effective way to increase engagement is by following others. On Tumblr, following matters less than other types of engagement, but it is still key.

- **Give Your Business Profile a Unique Look**: As popular as Facebook and Twitter are, apart from changing the cover and profile photo, there is not much to do to personalize the look of a profile. Tumblr is a completely different platform, as it supports custom modifications. Want to stand out from the crowd? Hire a designer or get a professional looking and flexible theme to make the most out of this branding opportunity. Adidas' Tumblr page is a great example of how a profile can be customized in order to imprint the brand in the customer's mind.

The sports apparel company is promoting more than just products on its Tumblr. It shares experiences and a lifestyle that's matching its products.

Figure 4.12: Tumblr page of Nike Women

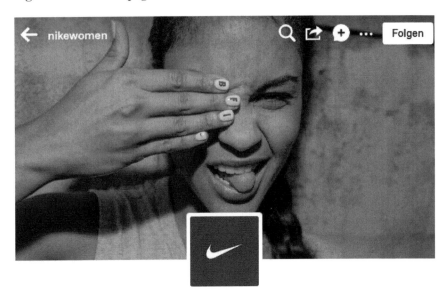

Source: https://bit.ly/35agH2Q; accessed 4th May 2020

4.3 Social Publishing Zone

Zone 2: Social Publishing sites help dissemination of content to an audience. The channels of social publishing include blogs, micro sharing sites, media sharing sites, and social bookmarking and news sites. Blogs are website and regularly updated online content, like an online journal, that includes chronological entries made by individuals. The word blog was derived from the combination of the word web and log. Blogs typically focus on a specific subject (economy, entertainment news, etc.) and provide users with forums (or a comment area) to talk about each posting. Many people use blogs as they would a personal journal or diary. Blogs are maintained by bloggers (individuals, journalists or organizations) and blogs feature a wide range of topics. Blogs are social because they are participatory and include the option for the reader to leave comments that can result in discussions related to specific posts.

Microblogging sites work like blogs except that there is often a limit to the length of the content users can post. Twitter (which is also a social community site) is the most well-known micro sharing site, which limits posts to 280 characters (please refer to the appropriate sections above).

In the following sections, we will further explore the most important platforms in the social publishing zone.

4.3.1 Instagram

Instagram is an online mobile photo-sharing app that allows its users to share pictures and videos either publicly or privately, as well as through a variety of other social networking platforms, such as Facebook, Twitter and Tumblr. Instagram was created by Kevin Systrom and Mike Krieger, and launched in October 2010 as a free mobile app. The company was acquired by Facebook in April 2012 for approximately US$1 billion in cash and stock.

The mobile-based photo- and video-sharing social network powers the sharing of images and creation of community among users around the world. At only seven years old in 2017, the platform has shown significant growth in its overall user base and in almost every demographic group. As people join Instagram in droves, brands have a unique opportunity for engagement with their fans. However, success for brands on Instagram takes more than publishing attractive images—it is the product of thoughtful strategy, a well-defined brand identity grounded in visual creativity and effective stakeholder management. As you explore the potential of Instagram for your business, keep in mind the specific strengths of visual media for telling a compelling story about your brand. When you put these principles into practice and combine storytelling with stunning images your brand will reap the benefits (Johnston, 2016).

In the next sections, we will show you how to create a compelling and sophisticated Instagram marketing strategy (Johnston, 2016).

Determine Your Objectives

Instagram's focus on visual sharing offers a unique platform to showcase your company and people as well as products and services. The mobile nature of the app lends itself to quickly capturing moments, giving followers an opportunity to interact with your brand in a way that can feel more casual and instantaneous than on other networks.

Depending on your industry, brand and key performance indicators, your specific Instagram strategy might target several of the following objectives (Johnston, 2016):

- Increase brand awareness
- Visualize company culture
- Showcase your team and recruit new talent
- Increase customer engagement and loyalty
- Showcase products and services
- Enhance and complement event experiences
- Incentivize consumer engagement with your brand
- Share company news
- Grow your community
- Connect with influencers
- Drive sales through a third-party app

Develop a Content Strategy

Content is the basis of your Instagram presence. Many B2C businesses (Business-to-Customer) use Instagram to make their product the star of the show, while B2B companies often focus on company culture and team recruitment. Based on your **target audience** and objectives, develop a plan to deliver eye-catching content to your community on a consistent and

compelling basis. It is recommendable to build **content themes** by reviewing your objectives and determine what aspects of your brand to showcase
in your Instagram content. Products, services, team members and culture all
offer rich potential for subject matter over time. Once you have a list of
definite content themes, brainstorm possible subjects for your images and
videos. Some companies focus on showcasing their products and services,
offering practical tutorials or going the opposite direction. For example,
Dunkin Donuts' colorful feed puts their offerings front and center, showing
off both standard and seasonal offerings by tying post content to major hol-
idays and events (Johnston, 2016).

Figure 4.13: adidas Football Instagram Account

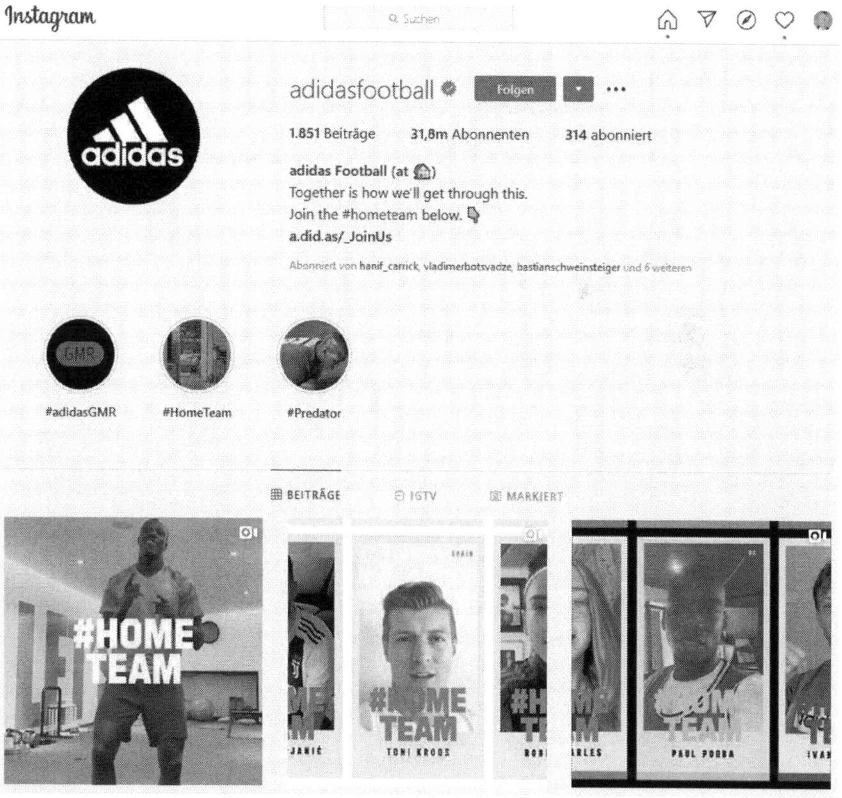

Source: https://bit.ly/2KHSc3D; accessed 4th May 2020

Determine Types of Content & Ratio

Instagram started as a photo-sharing app, but its wide and huge base of creative users publishes everything from videos to graphics to animated GIFs. As you plan your content, consider a balance of content types that will work best for the resources you have and the engagement you want from your audience. If video enables you to tell a compelling story about your product, work it into your content more often. Please note that in the above-mentioned example of Dunkin Donuts, videos received the most attention. If you don't have the resources - time, skills or comfort level - to execute video at the level you aspire, you may choose not to publish video at all or hire an appropriate agency to support your strategy. With composition for Instagram, quality matters, and it is worth spending the time to create the best possible content.

Beyond its flagship app, Instagram offers several supporting and **supplementary apps** that help you get even more creative with your posts. The suite of apps includes Hyperlapse, Layout and Boomerang, which empower users to create time-lapse video, image collages and GIFs, respectively. These additional apps allow brands and consumers alike to create more unique, Instagram-specific content even without in-house design or video production capabilities (Johnston, 2016).

Set a Content Calendar, but Remain Flexible

To establish and maintain an active presence on the platform, determine the frequency with which you will post. Then you should develop a content calendar that cycles through your themes and integrates key dates and respective campaigns. You should prepare content (photos, videos, captions) in advance and create a content calendar so that your team knows when posts should go live. Some of the best content for Instagram, however, will occur spontaneously, especially if your aim is to highlight company culture or events. By preparing content and setting a general schedule beforehand, you can allow the flexibility to take advantage of opportunities when they occur. During events, be ready to publish quickly to take advantage of real-time marketing and engagement (Johnston, 2016).

Curate User-Generated Content

If your Instagram community members are sharing their own content featuring your brand, you should capitalize on that. Curating content from your fans allows you to foster audience engagement and create an incentive for your audience to share their own creative ways of interacting with your brand, products or company.

As always, the pictures and videos you choose to curate should match your brand aesthetic. Make sure to review users' accounts and other posts before sharing their content to best judge whether it is appropriate to publicly align your brand with them by sharing their photo. In terms of best practices, it is courteous to ask someone for permission before sharing ('regramming') a photo. Pay attention to always give credit by @mentioning the original photographer in your caption, and provide your fans with insight on how to share more photos that your brand might feature in the future. You can find user-generated content on Instagram by monitoring your branded hashtags and business' locations (Johnston, 2016).

Establish Clear Guidelines for Your Team: Style, Publishing & Workflow

A consistent voice on social media is key to building your brand, especially on a visual platform such as Instagram. Even if one person is responsible for managing your brand's Instagram account, establishing guidelines for photo and video composition, filter use and captions will ensure that your content is part of a unified brand experience for your followers.

Create an Instagram Style Guide

Your style guide should outline your approach to each of the following (Johnston, 2016):

- **Brand aesthetic**: Review the existing visual representations of your brand: your logo, website, graphics and stock photography.

- **Composition**: While you can publish pictures with a landscape or portrait orientation to your Instagram feed, each piece of content will show up as a square thumbnail in your profile grid. You should determine your approach to a few basic elements of composition in order to create a sense of visual harmony when a user looks at your profile such as backgrounds, white space balance, dominant color(s) and subject.

- **Using Filters, Lux & Creative Tools**: Instagram offers several ways to edit photos and videos. Review filters and their effects to select a handful that fit your brand's aesthetic and ensure visually consistent and appealing content. For photo editing, you also have the option to apply Lux or use creative tools. Lux adjusts the contrast and saturation of your photo. Tools allows you to individually adjust brightness, contrast, warmth, shadows, color and more. For video editing, you can select a filter, trim content and choose a specific cover image that will show up in the news feed.

- **Captions**: Captions are limited to 2,200 characters and truncated with an ellipsis after three lines of text. While some users omit captions altogether, others approach sharing as a form of microblogging and write a short story to accompany every post. Make sure to include the most important part of your message within those first three lines. As with all aspects of style, consistency is key. Your guidelines should include whether sentence fragments are acceptable, if you plan to use emoji and hashtags (and how many to use in a given post), and what your policy is around @mentioning other users.

- **Hashtags**: Hashtags allow users to discover content and accounts to follow, so using them is a good way to connect with new followers and increase engagement on your posts. Instagram allows up to 30 hashtags per post or comment, so decide whether your brand will use them, how many to include in a typical post and whether you want to create branded hashtags to align with your content. Allow yourself some time to browse trending hashtags within the Instagram app's 'Search and Explore' tab to see what people are talking about and find opportunities for your brand to join relevant conversations. Some popular hashtags you can jump on are #insta-good, #instatravel, and #latergram. You may consider adding two or three relevant hashtags to your posts if suitable. Unlike other platforms, you can get away with adding more hashtags in a comment for more exposure. While it is tempting to plan all of your social posts in advance, joining trending conversations is a good way to connect with new audiences and stay true to the 'insta' part of this app.

- **Add to Photo Map**: Location tagging, or geo-tagging, using the 'Add to Photo Map' feature is another powerful way to increase engagement and allow new users to discover your content. Posts with a location receive a significantly higher engagement than posts without.
- **Tag People**: If you tag other Instagram users in a post, it will show up on their profile under the 'Photos of User' section. You can use this function to tag individuals or brands featured in your posts, and users will be able to tap your photo to view and click tagged handles.
- **Social Sharing**: Instagram allows you to connect your profile to other accounts such as Facebook, Twitter and Tumblr automatically push your photo to those networks. Determine whether you want to cross-post or promote your Instagram content in this way.

Identify Team Members & Roles

Your social media managers should be part of your Instagram marketing, but other team members may also provide valuable contributions.

Depending on your team and objectives, you might divide responsibilities into content creation and publishing, community management, discovery and analytics, and assign them to team members with different strengths.

For enterprises that require outbound message approval before publishing, establish a concise process for creating and reviewing content (Johnston, 2016).

Foster Engagement & Set Guidelines for Community Management

From curating user generated content to encouraging dialogue and building a community, Instagram offers tremendous potential for engagement with followers.

If you stick to publishing and skip engagement, you will miss out on a chance to organically grow your following by interacting with fans and reaching new audiences (Johnston, 2016):

- **Optimize Your Bio and Link**: With a 150-character limit, your Instagram bio should focus on what is most important about your company and brand. While users cannot click on hashtags in your bio, the way they can in captions, including a branded hashtag informs users how to share and find additional content related to your brand.
- **Following Accounts**: Following influencers in your industry - for example, if you are a clothing retailer, following top fashion bloggers - will help you keep an eye on interesting content and even find inspiration for your own posts. It helps to set basic guidelines around who your brand will and will not follow.
- **Managing Comments, @Mentions & Direct Messages**: If your brand receives a large volume of engagement, it can be difficult to ensure that no messages fall through the cracks. For those messages that have been identified to require a response, your team should have a plan in place for handling certain types of messages: Support or customer service inquiries, negative or disparaging comments, career inquiries, sales leads and spam. Some messages may require a reroute to another platform; for example, it may be easier to handle support issues via live chat, phone or email. Use Bitly or another link-shortening software tool to prepare an easy-to-remember short link to pages related to common inquiries.
  A common practice is to **@mention** other users - sometimes in a descriptive caption, sometimes in a comment - to give credit or draw their attention to a certain photo or video. If you receive notifications that your brand is @mentioned, it is always worth spending a moment to acknowledge an on-brand fan photo with a Like or a comment.

Instagram Direct allows users to send a photo or video directly to anyone. If a user sends this type of message to your handle, and you are not following them, the post will be in your requests queue, where you can accept their request to review and respond to their post. While some brands have successfully used Instagram Direct to collect user-submitted photos and reward fans, if these messages are not an essential part of your campaign or strategy, decide on a response procedure. In general, keeping interactions to public posts works best for most brands.

- **Monitoring Hashtags & Location Tags**: Another way to see who is talking about your brand, is to monitor branded hashtags. Those hashtags often include your brand name and any common misspellings; names of services, products, or events. You cannot control who will use your branded hashtags, so some posts may not be relevant, but monitoring the conversation will allow you to engage with followers who are sharing your brand with their networks. If certain locations are significant to your organization, regularly monitoring location tags will also help you identify users posting from those areas. When a location is tagged in a post, users can click on its name to see all photos tagged in that place from public accounts and private accounts that they are following – providing them with an overview of all content shared from a certain location.

Analyze Your Results

Tracking how well your content performs will allow you to adapt your Instagram marketing strategy over time. This allows you to deliver more of the content that your audience responds to while optimizing your plans for future marketing campaigns. When looking at your sent messages, analyzing the number of comments and likes received, as well as the engagement rate for each post, will show you how different types of content perform. The engagement rate is a percentage of likes plus comments on the post, divided by followers of the account at the time the post was sent.

Other metrics, such as overall follower count, branded hashtag mentions and location tags can give you a better idea of the results of your publishing and engagement efforts. Many companies also use a link to an Instagram-specific landing page or with a specific tag to track the number of clicks on the link in their profile.

As you develop and implement your brand's Instagram marketing strategy, you will find what types of content, workflow and engagement practices work best for you. Building your brand and growing a following can be challenging, but with the right strategy, you will be able to tell a powerful story and encourage increased engagement on the platform and beyond (Johnston, 2016).

4.3.2 Pinterest

Pinterest is a web and mobile application company, founded in 2010 by Ben Silbermann, Paul Sciarra and Evan Sharp, which operates a photo sharing website.

With the ever-growing list of social media sites available to run marketing campaign on, it is often difficult to choose which ones you want to prioritize. Facebook is almost always a given for brands to start with, and Instagram and Twitter are normally ranked high too. Nevertheless, Pinterest has also gained in popularity amongst marketers.

In the following paragraphs, we are going to provide you with a comprehensive step-by-step guide to Pinterest marketing which contains everything you need to build a strong content marketing presence on the platform - including how to get your individual pins noticed.

Why Consider Pinterest?

When considering what social media channels to use for your business in general and marketing in particular, Pinterest might not be at the top of your list. This is a missed opportunity as the network contains lots of creativity, eager customers, and those seeking ideas. Using Pinterest for business is the perfect way to get your product or service discovered by millions of people looking for things to plan, buy and do. As there are over 250 million Pinterest users seeking information, advice, and inspiration the network simply cannot be ignored (Fontein, 2016).

As Pinterest shares, about 67% of Pinners are under the age of 40. Even more interesting is the fact, that 54 percent of women aged 34 to 55 are on the site, and 35 percent of them have household incomes of over $100,000. If you're looking to target male-identified individuals, you might be surprised to learn that male users have grown 120 percent in 2016.

In addition, Pinners are open to your marketing: According to research from Ahalogy, Pinners are eager to connect with brands. When asked who they would rather follow - their favorite brand/store or celebrity - 83% of people said they would prefer to follow the former. This preference was true in a lot of retail categories, too, for example 73% of people said they would rather follow their favorite brand of beauty products than their favorite makeup artist (Fontein, 2016).

Because of this, Pinterest has influence on what people are actually buying. Using social media to research or bookmark items for purchase is a core element of the social buying process nowadays, and you can ensure your brand is involved by integrating Pinterest into your strategy. Why? According to Pinterest, 87% of Pinners have purchased a product because of Pinterest and 93% of Pinners have used Pinterest to plan a future purchase.

If your goal is to increase traffic to your website, Pinterest can also be a powerful lever as Pinterest states that about five percent of all website referral traffic comes from the site (second to only Facebook).

Pinterest functions differently than any of the other social media sites as for many Pinners, the idea is not necessarily so much to broadcast images or ideas to followers, but to save ideas, products, or content for later. This makes it a perfect marketing platform. Another key difference is that Pinterest displays content differently than any other social media site, and it does so in four ways. Users can view your pins (Gotter, 2016):

- On their home feed, if they follow you or the pins are deemed to be particularly relevant to their interests.
- By searching for a keyword relevant to your pin.

- In relevant categories (like 'Health and Fitness').
- On your actual profile, under themed/categorized boards.

This means that relevant, interested users can find your content organically, whether they are following you (or even know anything about you) or not.

Finally, the real strength of Pinterest is the integrated features of their business accounts. Join the 500,000 + businesses with Pinterest for Business accounts, and you will get added marketing features to promote your brand on one of the fastest growing social media platforms.

Setting Up Your Business Account and Profile

You might be using Pinterest for personal reasons already, but it could be time to create a **business account**. A business account has different terms of service than a personal account, so make sure you familiarize yourself with these.

When you go to create an account, you will see the option at the bottom of the sign in box to 'Continue as a Business.' If you miss it, you can still convert your account to a business later, but it is easier to do it right from the start. When you create your account as a business, you will be asked to fill out the additional fields supplying the information of your business's name, what type of business you are, and your website (though this is optional). Once you have created your account you will be then be asked to follow 5 topics that interest you. This does not really matter, since you will be using this primarily to promote your content instead of following others, but it never hurts to select topics that are relevant to your business (Gotter, 2016; Fontein, 2016; Daley, 2015).

When you click on the red thumb tack in the top right-hand corner you get to your **profile**. Edit it accordingly and give as much information as you can - users will see this, and the more info, the better. Choose an image that best represents your brand; in most cases this is your logo. Make sure to add your website so users can visit you through it. Locations matter if you are a local or brick-and-mortar location, and always try to use keywords in your 'about me' section. Once your profile has been set up, you can start creating your boards.

Setting Up Boards

You can create a board from your profile page. You will be asked to name it, describe it, what category it falls under, if it is secret, and if you want to invite collaborators. When you name your board, keep keywords in mind, and make sure it is a relevant title as it could help your search results and help you connect with more relevant users. The description matters just as much as the title so use keywords and describe it accurately. Once you add pins to the board, you can choose which image you want to represent the board. You can go to 'edit board', and then choose to change your cover image as appropriate (Gotter, 2016; Fontein, 2016; Daley, 2015).

Viewing Analytics

Pinterest has their own analytics program, available only for business accounts. You can view the analytics by clicking on the tab on the navigation bar in the top left hand corner of the page. Pinterest's analytics can tell you how many views and how much engagement your pins and boards are getting, along with information about your followers or those who viewed your pins.

When you first access Pinterest's Analytics, you'll be taken right to your dashboard. On your dashboard, you will be able to see a quick overview of what's going on with your profile, including (Gotter, 2016; Fontein, 2016; Daley, 2015):

- Number of average daily impressions
- Average daily viewers
- Amount of average monthly viewers
- Average monthly engaged
- Top pin impressions in the past 30 days (which will show you the amount of impressions, repins, clicks, and likes those pins have)

On the right-hand side of the page, you'll see a box that says 'What to see more?' Once you confirm your website by installing a code they give you into your website index, you will be able to know what all your content is doing on Pinterest - not just the pins you have actually pinned.

In any case, it is instrumental to know who your audience is and how your profile is performing, in the most amount of detail as possible. By looking at your audience analytics and comparing it to your audience on other platforms, you can see who you are missing. Sometimes the answer will be that a large percentage of that demographic just does not frequently use Pinterest; sometimes, though, you may be missing them for another reason. In this case, you can either create new pins, boards, and content to try to engage with them.

Analytics can also help you to gear more content towards the audience that you do have on Pinterest. In a lot of cases, the audience you have on Pinterest may not be identical to the one you have on Facebook or Twitter or YouTube.

How to Create Popular Pins

While setting up your profile in a way that is optimized for success is important, your actual pins will be what matters most. Your pins need to be visually appealing so they stand out against the others, whether that is in a page of other search results or under a general category. There are several ways you can get your pins noticed and increase their visibility, in addition to choosing the right keywords to describe them (Gotter, 2016; Fontein, 2016; Daley, 2015; Kawasaki and Fitzpatrick, 2014):

- **Best Image Size**: Choosing the right image size on Pinterest can help your pin stand out from the rest, regardless of where users are viewing it. Image on Pinterest will be scaled to fit the platform, with the width being scaled to 236 pixels. By Pinterest's own recommendations, the best aspect ratios for Pins fall between a 2:3 and 1:3.5 (width to height). The minimum recommended width is 600 pixels. Having Pins that are taller than they are wide can help your pins have enough space to stand out, but pins that seem to go on forever and are too long do not get nearly as much engagement.

- **Tasteful branding**: According to Pinterest, including 'tasteful branding' in the image can help increase repins and engagement, which can lead to purchases. Whether this is featuring the packaging of your product in the image or just a small logo or watermark, they recommend adding it in where possible.

- **Add lifestyle images**: While images of your products alone can be effective, adding in lifestyle images where users are actively using your product or service can help it get the attention of users but avoid overly user-generated images.

- **Best Times to Pin**: The best times to pin depend on your target audience's habits, so you should always test for your specific optimal posting times. But, for your general information, according to SocialFresh, on average, the best times to post are 2PM – 4PM EST and 8PM – 1AM EST; and, research by HubSpot says Saturday morning is THE best time to post.

- **Make It Easy to Pin Content from Your Sites**: Add a hovering Pin It button to any image on any of your sites or your phone app through Pinterest directly. Or, if you use WordPress, there is a Pinterest Pin It Hover button plugin. These simple-to-integrate buttons direct your site visitors to either check out your Pinterest account or actually pin your site's content on their own accounts.

- **Connect with Your Other Social Media Platforms**: You do not want to have to start over with followers when you create a new social media account. It is easy to connect your Twitter and Facebook accounts to your Pinterest for Business account. This will help you get more followers by tapping into the ones you already have on other platforms. It also will help spread your content across platforms. And, it will add Twitter and Facebook buttons to your Pinterest account.

- **Share Pins in Your Newsletter**: Take the difficulty out of getting people to find your pins by sending the pins straight to them! Your newsletter is the perfect place to throw in a couple of your latest pins and direct subscribers to your Pinterest account.

- **Study Pinterest's categories**: Pinterest users can search the network for content in many different categories. Get to know the ones that apply to your business to determine where your content fits. Some of the top pinned categories include 'home décor', 'food and drink', 'DIY', and crafts. Once you figure out the categories that apply to your business, remember to categorize any pin board you create to make it easier for users to discover your content.

- **Post Frequently**: To get more Pinterest followers, you should post frequently, at least once a day. Make sure you are not just repinning the content of others, but also pinning your own unique pins with your own content. Avoid pinning all new pins within a 5-minute span but spread your pinning throughout the day.

- **Create appealing content you can Pin:** Like most social networks, you want your business' Pinterest profile to be a mix of original and curated content - with an emphasis on articles and photos pinned from your site. Pinners love learning new ways of doing things, and you have a unique opportunity to share knowledge about your area of expertise. Share tutorials and how-to articles in order to teach users something new, or use your own expertise to offer advice. Another type of content that often makes it to the top Pinned lists is infographics. Start by finding and repinning well-researched and well-designed infographics on the topics relevant to your field. Mercedes, for instance, is a great example how appealing content may look like. They have dozens of different pin boards covering very diverse aspects of their products and service and wider thematic areas such as their 'Taste for Adventure' pin board which features great content and appealing visuals as to their SUVs and sports cars.

- **Engage with Followers and Reply to Comments**: Just like you respond to tweets, Facebook posts, and Instagram comments, engage with your followers directly by answering their questions and responding to their comments. Go the extra mile and address them directly, using their names to really take your customer service to the next level. Engagement is a two-way street. You need to reach out to your followers' boards as well so leave comments on their pins so they will feel appreciated and recognized. Their followers will see your brand, too!

- **Follow and Engage with Popular Boards**: The best way to see successful Pinterest strategy in action is to follow and engage with popular boards. You can learn a lot and see what kinds of pins they pin, what kinds of boards they have, and how much engaging they do. Your goal is to get on that level! If you are commenting on these popular pins, your brand name will be seen by the huge number of people who follow those boards. It is a good idea to follow popular boards which are relevant to your industry. Another great board feature for marketing is the 'Open Board', which allows users to contribute their own pins. All you have to do is give them pinning access by adding their name or email. This feature is great for marketing because you get your community involved in a personal way so do invite your followers and get recognition boost if you can get industry experts and leaders to contribute to your boards!

- **Build Influencer Relationships**: Reach a wider audience and gain more followers by reaching out to influencers in your field. Start by following their boards, repinning their pins, and leaving engaging comments on their pins. Once you have dropped your name that way, you can initiate a n intensified collaboration and ask if they will post on a board of yours, or offer to contribute to one of their boards. Offer ideas for their boards and show that you are familiar with their content when initiating collaboration.

- **Find Friends from Other Social Media Platforms**: You know that when you create a new account with Instagram or another social media platform, they ask if you want to 'Find Friends' using your phone's contacts or Facebook friends. Do not waste all the Twitter and Facebook contacts you may have created. Follow them, and they will find you! The Find Friends button is in the upper-left corner of your Pinterest home page.

- **Add CTAs (Call to Action) to your Descriptions**: Encouraging users to 'click to learn more' or 'sign up now' can be enough to actually inspire action. Call to action pins can increase engagement and conversions substantially.

- **Hold a contest**: Contests are a great way to boost engagement, drive sales, and involve your followers in your product or service. However, if you post a contest on Facebook with the intention of directing your followers to Pinterest, your contest can hold a larger significance.

- **Capitalize on Keywords**: If you're posting timely content that's relevant based on a specific event, holiday, or season, users might come to Pinterest searching for it. You want to ensure your pin is the one that pops up when they hit enter on that search button. A deliberate use of keywords will support this goal. Keywords are just as important on pins as they are on blog posts. Pinterest's search engine is frequently used by pinners who are looking for specific content, and you want to make sure that yours is what you find. Having relevant, timely content is a great way to help you rank well in a lot of searches, as there will be a surge of interested users looking for your content at exactly the right time.

Pinterest's Promoted Pins

Pinterest's Promoted Pins is their paid ad platform. It works on a bidding system like the other social media ad platforms. You pay to have your pin placed in front of your target audience. Your pins will show up in relevant category feeds and relevant searches, aided by the keywords that you choose (Gotter, 2016; Fontein, 2016; Daley, 2015).

To access the promoted pins platform, click on the 'Ads' clickable tab and drop down menu, which can be located in the left-hand corner. This will take you to the dashboard, where you can see the total number of impressions, engagement, conversions, and ad spend on all your campaigns in the prior week. This information can be further broken down by engagement campaigns and traffic campaigns.

If you want to create an ad you will be first be asked to decide whether you want to boost engagement with your pins, which will focus on and charge by close-up views, repins, and clicks, or send traffic to your site, which will charge by clicks. Once you choose your campaign goal, you will add in information about your campaign name, your daily budget, and the start and end date for your campaign.

When you have filled out all the information, click 'Pick a Pin' and select the pin you want to promote. When choosing a pin, you can search for a pin by the keyword or URL, or scroll through your pins. You can see the number of repins each has as you scroll through them. Pinterest also gives you the option of viewing your most clicked and most repined pins in the past 30 days (Gotter, 2016; Fontein, 2016; Daley, 2015).

On the next screen, you should give your promoted pin its name, which will be the visible title of the pin that users will see. You can also set a destination URL.

Below this, you will be able to select different interests, which are used as a sort of targeting criteria. These interests will help reach a relevant audience in their browsing and home feeds. They will also sort your post into the correct categories. When you scroll down, you will be asked to choose appropriate keywords. The keywords you choose will determine what searches your pin shows up in. You want to connect with users who are actively searching for content like yours. Pinterest automatically suggests searches based on their information about your pin, and they will provide a list of keywords for every search that you make. Click on different keywords to add them to your campaign. We recommend using 20-30 keywords per promoted pin. When it comes to the keywords you choose, think outside of the box to help your pin show up in more searches (Gotter, 2016; Fontein, 2016; Daley, 2015).

When you scroll to the next section, you can have your pins only shown to those (Gotter, 2016):

- in certain locations
- who speak certain languages
- use specific devices
- are a certain gender

Next, you will be able to set your maximum CPC bid which is the most you are willing to pay for a single click to your website (or, in the case of an engagement objective, for a single measure of engagement). This must be at least $0.10. Pinterest will let you know if your bid is too high or low compared to what others are bidding.

Once you submit your campaign, it will need to pend until approval. You can view your campaigns' approval status under the engagement campaigns or traffic campaigns tabs. Both as your campaigns progress and once they are over, it important to monitor them through the promoted pins analytics. You can find information about how your campaigns are performing on the home page of the ads platform, or find detailed information on each campaign by clicking on them (Gotter, 2016).

Figure 4.14: Rolex Pinterest Account

ROLEX

✔ 806Tsd. monatliche Betrachter

🌐 www.rolex.com

A symbol of perpetual excellence, Rolex watches are precise, reliable and built to last. Explore the inspiring collection.

Source: https://www.pinterest.de/rolex/; accessed 4th May 2020

Pinterest's Buyable Pins

Promoted Pins are doing exceptionally well, and buyable pins are driving major conversions. Promoted Pins allow businesses to guarantee that users are seeing their pins. Buyable pins enable users to purchase directly off of a pin, without ever leaving Pinterest. Pinterest's buyable pins are a simple, fast, and secure way for users to make purchases. Buyable pins are identifiable to users by a 'Buy It' tag that shows up right next to the 'Pint it' button. Users can see the price of the item, and will be taken through a swift check out process, all on Pinterest. As users are browsing through Pinterest, creating their wish lists and getting ideas, they will be able to see your product, the price, and purchase it all with a few quick taps or clicks on their mobile device. They do not even repeatedly enter in their payment information, making the process go swiftly - before they get the chance to talk themselves out of it (Gotter, 2016).

Pinterest's Rich Pins

Pinterest's Rich Pins are Pins that include extra information right on the Pin itself. There are 6 types of Rich Pins: app, movie, recipe, article, product and place. When you apply for Rich Pins, you'll get real-time information automatically updated on your pins and more ways to direct people to your site because your site will be linked to your Rich Pins (Gotter, 2016; Daley, 2015).

For any of your Rich Pins to have even the potential to direct traffic to your site, you need to get them validated on the Pinterest site itself (Gotter, 2016; Daley, 2015):

- Go to the Pinterest developers page
- Decide what kind of Rich Pin you want to apply for
- Read the documentation for your Rich Pin type
- Add the appropriate meta tags to your site
- Validate your Rich Pins and apply to get them approved

Once your Rich Pins are approved by Pinterest, they will be out there for the entire Pinterest world to see, to repin, and to be directed to your site!

Figure 4.15: Rich Pin from Ikea Canada on Pinterest

Source: https://bit.ly/2KSihxj; accessed 4th May 2020

4.3.3 SlideShare

SlideShare is a media-sharing site where users can upload files privately or publicly in the following file formats: PowerPoint, PDF, Keynote or Open-Document presentations. Launched on October 4, 2006, the website is similar to YouTube, but for slideshows. It was acquired by LinkedIn in 2012.

The platform also provides users the ability to rate, comment on, and share the uploaded content. Some of the notable users include 'The White House', 'NASA', 'World Economic Forum' and IBM.

According to the company, the platform has over 18 million uploads in 40 content categories which makes it one of the top 100 most-visited websites in the world. Consequently, it has been named 'the quiet giant of Content Marketing' as SlideShare is a crowded site with a highly-targeted audience and low competition which makes it a powerful tool to grow your business.

You can use SlideShare for many purposes. For instance, you can (D'Andrea, 2012):

- Get traffic
- Rank better on Google
- Grow your followers
- Get email subscribers
- Build your brand
- Create your own uses

If you use SlideShare in the right way, you will find it is a very powerful tool. Let us get into how you can take full advantage of this platform.

Setting Up Your Profile

When you sign up for an account, you will be given a choice to select the type of account you would like to create which is either a 'company/university/conference' or a 'LinkedIn' account.

As the platform was acquired by LinkedIn, you either have to set up an appropriate account or use your LinkedIn account to utilize SlideShare. Take some time when providing all the necessary information and use the same information and pictures you are using on other sites to reinforce your brand image (Zarella, 2010).

How to Make Astonishing Presentations

As with YouTube, watching a presentation is an attention-consuming task, so do not waste your viewer's time. Keep your slideshows as short a possible while still including value-adding information. People are just one click away from another presentation, so if you do not get their attention quickly, you will not get a second chance.

Figure 4.16: Appealing title and visuals pay off on SlideShare

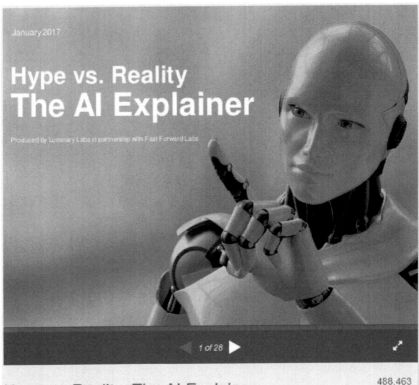

Hype vs. Reality: The AI Explainer

Source: https://bit.ly/2Yc0vg9; accessed 4th May 2020

Your presentations must be magnets and should grab people's attention from the start to the end. To make an appealing presentation, follow these following steps (Zarella, 2010; D'Andrea, 2012; Kawasaki and Fitzpatrick, 2014):

- **Work on Your Content**: The content always make the difference between good results and great results. Thus, insert something worth talking about in your slides. You have the options to show something amazing, explain and provide useful information and/or evoke emotions. These are the three kinds of content that perform best on SlideShare. Once you chose your topic, think about a great title. Your title has to seduce people to watch your presentation, or they will shift their attention to something else. The title also will become the URL your viewers will use to find your slides. Keep the title short and include appropriate keywords. Also, provide a summary of your presentation in the description section.

- **Construct a Clear and Linear Structure**: It is paramount that you construct a clear and linear structure for your presentation. Think of your presentation like an engine: if one piece is broken, the engine will not work properly or will not work at all! Forget about complex structures but think of a way to present your content like a list or a story. They are the best ways to deliver your message.
- **Create Powerful Slides**: Most people do not spend enough attention and time on design when they make their presentations. This is the reason you will see many presentations on SlideShare which are not appealing.

How to Increase Your Reach on SlideShare

Once you have designed your presentation, you have to upload it on SlideShare and promote it. Here are some suggestions for promoting your presentation effectively and increase your reach (Zarella, 2010; D'Andrea, 2012; Kawasaki and Fitzpatrick, 2014):

- **Share it on Your Blog**: You also want to insert your presentation in your blog to increase the number of views it gets.
- **Insert a URL**: Insert a URL in your call to action. Given that people are engaged when they watch a great presentation, the best place in which you can insert your link and still keep getting clicks is your last slide. If your presentation resonates with people, many of them will click on your link. In addition, if you want to grow your followers, just ask people to follow you on Twitter or other social media platforms by inserting the appropriate call to action at the end of your presentation. In the same way, you can ask people to like your Facebook Page, to add you to their circles on Google Plus, to follow you on Pinterest, and so on.

- **Embed self-explanatory text**: Whereas the optimal format for PowerPoint is slides with minimal text accompanied by an oral explanation, the optimal format for SlideShare is slides with self-explanatory text, because that is the only explanation most SlideShare users will ever see.

- **Create a Compelling Title Page**: Another difference between SlideShare and PowerPoint you should be aware of in order to increase your reach on SlideShare is that a SlideShare presentation requires a much better title page than a PowerPoint presentation. Whereas hardly anyone pay attention to the title page of a PowerPoint presentation, the title page of a SlideShare presentation must immediately inspire people to click through.

- **Share it on other social media platforms**: You have a good reason to share your presentations on other social media platforms such as Facebook, Twitter, Plus and LinkedIn: If you get enough views on it, your presentation will be shown at the top of SlideShare's homepage (Figure 4.17).

Figure 4.17: 'Today's Top SlideShares' section on SlideShare

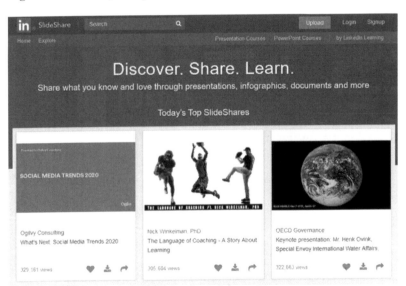

Source: https://www.slideshare.net/; accessed 4th May 2020

4.3.4 Internet Forums

Forums are arguably the oldest type of social media and a modern version of community bulletin boards. The focus of these kinds of sites is discussion. Users will make posts to them and others will respond. Forum marketing is a great way to make your online business stand out from the crowd. Forum users are generally open to making online purchases. In addition, forum users are often also respected experts and bloggers in the specific topics covered by the forum. Against this background, it is instrumental for you to become a valuable and respected member in appropriate communities by answering questions and contributing useful information. Forum marketing is a high ROI strategy because making a sophisticated impression in front of this influential audience can help your marketing message spread far and wide (Zarella, 2010).

Unlike other types of social media, where there are a few major sites, there are thousands of popular forums on the Web, each focused on a single topic or community. Consequently, it is key for you to find the ones that are relevant to your business and engage them.

Follow this step-by-step guide to effectively use forum marketing as a part of your overall social media marketing strategy and avoid some common mistakes (Go, 2016).

Find the Right Forums for Your Market Niche

Not all forums are worth your time and budget. Successful forum marketing first means finding the right community for your business. Look for popular forums that cover your specific topic. Start by asking your employees, suppliers, and customers which online communities – if any - they hang out in.

In addition, try doing a simple Google search for a keyword related to your niche plus 'forum'.

While you will probably come across hundreds, and possibly thousands of forums, you must narrow your list to 5-10 forums that will be worth your time using the following criteria (Go, 2016):

- Ideally, look for forums that have at least 1,000 members and 10,000 posts.
- Make sure the forum gets at least ten to fifteen new posts on a daily basis.
- Ignore forums that are overrun by spam.
- For competitor analysis reason also include forums hosted by your direct competitors

In order to asses and analyze the different forums and get a sound overview you can refer to respective internet websites such as Alexa. This website provides an in-depth analysis of thousands of different forums which can be browsed by category.

The following figure, for example, shows the highest ranked forums in the area of 'Internet Marketing' (Figure 4.18).

Figure 4.18: Alexa as an Internet Forum search tool

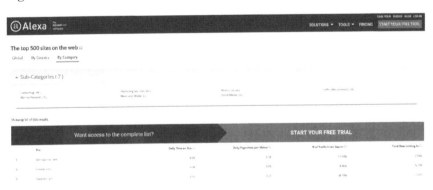

Source: https://bit.ly/2SdRWxG; accessed 4th May 2020

Furthermore, there are also traffic statistics provided such as monthly unique visitor metrics, audience geography, daily pageviews per visitor and also which search keywords send traffic to this site!

Create Your Online Forum Account

Once you identified the forums you would like to consider for your online marketing, you shall setup your forum accounts right away. Your profile in a forum is a representation of who you are (Go, 2016).

Seniority is important in appropriate forum communities. Users with older registration dates are usually given more deference than more recent users. Some forums even prevent new users from posting for the first few days after their initial registration. Given the great advantage of early registration, you should create your forum accounts as soon as possible.

Effective forum marketing means that it is part of your long-term strategy. You should think of forums as a permanent marketing channel for your business, instead of just one of many targets to boost your new advertising campaign (Go, 2016).

The most important part of profile setup is your avatar which is an image that will be displayed next to every post you make, so choose it wisely and in accordance with your avatars set for the other social media platforms. If your account will represent you personally, you should choose the same good personal photo you use for YouTube, Twitter and other platforms. Otherwise, you should make you avatar an extension of the brand you are promoting e. g. by using a logo. Include URL and social media links and – if applicable - explain what your business does in a few sentences (Go, 2016).

Your username and avatar are the first things other users will notice about you so do pick a username that is easy to remember and pronounce. Using your real name might be appropriate, especially if your name is closely identified with your brand. Refrain from using number combination or weird misspellings.

A sophisticated profile can support you establish credibility on the forum so provide a solid description of your expertise and experience. Stay away from sharing potentially polarizing information such as political affiliation. Provide contact information so other users can get in touch with you if they are interested in learning more about your business. As a lot of spammers search through forums for personal information you should only share information you would not mind being made public. Most forums today will allow you to post links to your Facebook page, LinkedIn profile, Twitter account along with other social media account such as Pinterest and Instagram - be sure to utilize these platforms and link to them!

Check the Community Guidelines Before Posting

During the registration process, you will be asked to agree to the forum's user agreement and posting guidelines. Read these rules and guidelines very carefully. Some of the most important issues to look for include (Go, 2016):

- Are users allowed to place links in their posts?
- Are users allowed to promote their own businesses?
- Are users allowed to post commercial messages?
- Are users allowed to contact other members for commercial purposes?
- What restrictions are placed on new users?
- What special privileges are given to veteran users?

Violating any of these rules can quickly get you on the wrong side of the community members and completely invalidate your efforts of building veritable relationships, trust, and credibility with the forum community.

Introduce Yourself to the Community

Many forums encourage new users to introduce themselves to the community by making an initial introductory post. This is usually done in threads especially designated for welcoming new members. These threads are typically called some variation of 'Say Hi Here', 'How Did You Find Us', or 'New Members Check In Here.' Your introductory post should include a brief sketch of your expertise and an explanation of why you joined the forum. Let other users know that your main goal is to contribute to and learn from the community. Do not make any marketing pitches in your initial post. If you try to sell anything in your first post you will very likely get banned or ignored. Always keep in mind that it is all about joining the community, being helpful, and adding value, not selling (Go, 2016).

Spend Some Time 'Lurking' on the Forum

Resist the urge to start posting right away. Forums are strong communities that may tend to shun newcomers so spend some time reading the forum to get a sense of the community's special tonality and cultural norms. Figure out who the influential users are and note which topics are popular. Learning this information will help you fit in more effectively and efficiently. You will also get a lot of valuable insight into what the most common questions are in your market, what problems people have, and what are the most common types of solutions. From a marketing research perspective, this is invaluable data (Go, 2016).

Make Valuable and Useful Contributions to the Community in the Form of Posts

A post is traditionally a short text-based piece of content, but some types of forum allow you to upload and attach images as well. Your posts will be labelled with the date and time of creation, as well as the poster's username, avatar, and possibly some kind of reputation value. By all means, pay attention to making valuable and useful contributions to the community. Whenever anyone asks a question related to your products or services, provide swift and value-adding answers. These situations are opportunities to demonstrate your expertise and to build reputation and trust. If applicable, backup your advice with links to trusted sources, and respond to follow up questions as soon as possible (Go, 2016; Zarella, 2010; Kawasaki and Fitzpatrick, 2014). Like stated many times before, leave out your sales pitch in the beginning. Any hint of bias in your initial posts will erase all your work. By keeping your answers objective, the community will start thinking of you as a trusted expert. They will start asking you for your recommendations. When you get direct inquiries for recommendations you may then mention your business without appearing biased. Conversations on forums are organized into threads, with posts listed in chronological order from earliest to most recent.

The first post is usually called the original post (OP) is at the top of the thread, with response posts listed below. Forums are divided into categories, and threads are listed on each category's page, with the threads that have had new posts most recently at the top. When replying to a thread, stay relevant to the original post. Changing the topic or point of a thread is known as 'thread hijacking' and is frowned upon (Go, 2016; Zarella, 2010; Kawasaki and Fitzpatrick, 2014).

Against this background, search the forum for similar posts to ensure you are not duplicating and existing thread.

Put Your Website URL in Your Signature File

Forum signatures are blocks of text or graphic that are attached to the end of your posts. Most people use signatures to provide links to their favorite websites. Some forums also allow users to use signatures to promote their own websites. If that is the case, make sure you take full advantage of this opportunity and create a forum marketing signature that works. Do not mishandle this opportunity by putting flashy images or long advertising messages in your signature. An accurate, short description of your business and a link to your website is the best option.

Over time as you produce more posts you will automatically have more chances for people to see your signature and drive traffic to your website (Go, 2016; Zarella, 2010; Kawasaki and Fitzpatrick, 2014).

Avoid Controversy and Drama in Online Forums

Do not get drawn into any arguments involving politics, religion, and other heated topics. Keep these things in mind before posting or responding to posts (Go, 2016; Zarella, 2010; Kawasaki and Fitzpatrick, 2014):

- Constantly remind yourself that your mission is to build good will for your company and business.
- Stay away from charged topics like politics or religion.
- Resist the immediate urge to respond to criticism. If you have to answer, at least give yourself a couple of hours to cool down before responding.
- Do not use emoticons unless this is in line with the tonality of your usual communication strategy.
- End discussions the moment you sense that it is getting contentious. Just say you agree to disagree and that you want to move on to other more pleasant topics.

Create Win-Win Marketing Campaigns

Once you have the respect of other users you can start to focus on marketing techniques that provide a benefit for the forum community. For example, offer the forum members special discounts, free samples, or run contests. Be sure to get the permission of the forum's moderators in advance before you start these campaigns (Go, 2016; Zarella, 2010; Kawasaki and Fitzpatrick, 2014).

Be Careful When Outsourcing Forum Marketing

Many companies use social bots or external staff to do forum marketing. This can be dangerous and counterproductive as this may result into spam which can then seriously damage your online reputation. When you hire a social media marketing manager, make sure they understand that you will only accept ethical marketing practices that will enhance your image (Go, 2016).

4.3.5 YouTube

YouTube is an American video-sharing website headquartered in California. It was acquired by Google in November 2006 for US$ 1.65 billion. YouTube now operates as one of Google's subsidiaries. The site allows the users to upload, view, rate, share, comment and add to favorites. Available content includes video clips, TV show clips, music videos, short and documentary films, audio recordings, movie trailers and other content such as video blogging, short original videos, and educational videos (Agrawal, 2017).

Most of the content on YouTube has been uploaded by individuals, but media corporations including BBC, CBS and Vevo offer some of their material via YouTube as part of the YouTube partnership program. YouTube earns advertising revenue from Google AdSense, a program which targets ads according to site content and audience. The clear majority of its videos are free to view, but there are exceptions, including subscription-based premium channels, film rentals, as well as YouTube Red, a subscription service offering ad-free access to the website and access to exclusive content made in partnership with existing users (Young, 2013).

YouTube has changed rapidly in its first 12 years. In its early days, it supported musicians and replaced MySpace as the platform for aspiring artists who posted their new compositions in search for followers and a record deal. For example, in January 2007, Justin Bieber's mother posted the first of many YouTube videos of her 12-year son singing R&B hits. He was discovered by a record company later that year, and got a record deal.

Today, YouTube is a huge video sharing platform that has everything from entertainment to informative lectures on many topics. In average a third of all internet users now watch online video every day. The platform opened the doors for a new self-invented type of celebrity – the YouTuber – and new entertainment formats. Old-style celebrities broadcasted to the masses from a TV studio, but typically remained distant. YouTubers, by contrast seek an intimate dialogue by narrowcasting from their private rooms. YouTubers try to set up their own business as media entrepreneurs. As members of the YouTube partner programme, they stand to make money from the numbers of views from the pre-roll ads before their videos. A few make a lot of money from both ad revenue and endorsements. However, for most the revenues are modest, but a welcome contribution for covering the expenses.

YouTube has been central to this change in media culture and consequently it has also awakened plenty of competition, with for example Facebook and Snapchat both energetically have developed their online video offer. However, YouTube has evolved to more than just 'the latest online videos'. Today, it is the world's largest and most up-to-date library of culture. A new type of entertainment has been invented as well. Superstar YouTubers, like PewDiePie (explained below), show themselves playing video games and give tips for gaming success to their followers. YouTube is also a huge archive for old films and video and it is evolving into a seemingly limitless archive and a global 'everything' channel. It continues to innovate and evolve.

Furthermore, YouTube has enriched modern search culture through the growing expectation that it holds a 'how to' video on almost anything: How to cook lasagne, how to put on make-up and how to perform a DIY task, such as how to shift a thermostat in your refrigerator. New products get reviewed on YouTube within days of launch. Running your own YouTube channel is a big commitment. It requires investment and time. Here are some of the brands and companies that should evaluate the opportunity to integrate YouTube as a way to influence customers. Constantly remind yourself that your mission is to build good will for your company and business (Agrawal, 2017; Young, 2013; Siu, 2016; Saunders, 2016):

- **Brands in high interest categories (such as automotive, travel, food, luxury, technology, fashion):** These, of course, also have information-hungry audiences, so brands can build trust and credibility by providing knowledge. For example, a glimpse behind the scenes at one of the great fashion shows (in New York, London, Paris or Milan) fascinates large numbers of young women. Popular and well-made videos perform well in search results which can increase a brand's engagement among all stakeholders (such as staff, trade customers) as well as 'mental availability' for potential buyers and those actively considering a purchase.
- **Gaming brands and new technologies:** YouTube is home to many influencers in tech and gaming – positive reviews from the likes of PewDiePie can help launch and popularize a new game.

PewDiePie is the pseudonym for Felix Arvid Ulf Kjellberg, who is a Swedish web-based comedian and video producer. Since August 2013 PewDiePie has been one of the most subscribed users on YouTube. In March 2017, the channel had 54 million subscribers. The focus of PewDiePie's YouTube videos is his commentary and reactions to various games as he plays through them. Due to this, his videos fall under the Let's Play umbrella.

- **Brands targeting Millennials and Gen Z:** YouTube has a broad user base, yet the heavy usage is among Millennials. YouTubers look and feel like representatives of the Millennial and Gen Z; they 'connect' with them in a way that few brands can emulate. This is 'their' channel – not that of their parents.

- **Brands that wish to be seen as experts:** In some categories (home improvement, technology and beauty are good examples) there is a hunger for advice and information. YouTube has evolved into a search engine and people increasingly turn to it for a 'how to' film, for example 'how to do my hair in the style of Game of Thrones'. Brands can be the providers of expert answers and increase their credibility and trust among potential buyers.

- **B2B marketers – especially professional services:** 'Thought leadership' is how many professional service companies build their brand reputation through being recognized as an authority in a specialized field. High tech firms often publish white papers with analysis of the economic benefits of their products as a form of marketing. YouTube help such B2B companies to project thought leadership in easier-to-consume short video formats. For example, by videoing conferences and webcasts, companies can generate informative short films about 'white papers' that can reach a wider audience over time – it is often a good idea to post edited highlights rather than the full version.

- **Companies who think they might negatively affected by ad blocking:** Consumers are increasingly choosing not to look at ads with ad blocking being highest among the young. Thus, video content (if it is regarded as useful or entertaining) can be an effective way to engage with online audiences. It 'bypasses' adblocking software as people choose to watch it and so value it more.

- **Companies looking to be truly customer-centric:** Companies have to be really tuned in to the daily needs and interests of their customers if they are to win audiences in the competitive and constantly changing market for online video. They must be constant creators (rather than occasional campaigners) because the setting up of a YouTube channel creates the expectation that fresh video will be posted regularly.

In future, we will probably see even more new brands being created and marketed by groups of YouTubers and man-aged by their agents, who understand the value of a strong supporters and subscribers on the YouTube channel.

Exhibit 4.5

Orabrush – how Procter & Gamble's 'pull' B2C YouTube marketing strategy helped consumers to be aware of the 'bad breath' problem

There are billions of bacteria on our tongue. These microbes that live in the mouth – on the tongue - are the main reasons for halitosis (bad breath), in about 80-90 percent of all cases. The tongue brushes/scrapers segment accounts for less than 1 percent of the total world oral care market. The world market for oral care is dominated by huge multinationals like Procter & Gamble (e.g. Oral-B), Colgate-Palmolive, GlaxoSmithKline, Unilever, Johnson & Johnson (e.g. Listerine) and Church & Dwight.

In an effort to make consumers' oral care routines more complete, some competitors have released new and unique products to help fill in the market niches, which are not currently covered by the big ones, like Colgate-Palmolive, Procter & Gamble, GlaxoSmithKline, Johnson & Johnson, Unilever and Church & Dwight. One of the companies that has seen success with this niche strategy is Orabrush (www.orabrush.com), which has cleverly combined its products with a clear social media strategy.

With this strategy, they have been able to occupy a segment in the market (tongue cleaning), which did not receive much attention by the multinationals until now. Using the social media (specifically YouTube and Facebook) Orabrush has turned tongue cleaning into just another step in consumers' pursuit of total oral care. Around late 2008, the 75-year-old inventor of the Orabrush and a former biochemist, Dr. Bob Wagstaff, had spent 8 years trying to bring Orabrush to market. He had spent over $40,000 on an infomercial. It only sold about 100 orders. He approached Walmart, Walgreens and many others, but no one was interested in his tongue cleaner. He approached Oral-B and Colgate-Palmolive asking if they wanted to buy his patent. They were not interested.

Figure 4.19: Orabrush product

Source: https://www.orabrush.com/orabrush/; accessed 4th May 2020

In 2009, as a last attempt, Dr. Bob went to the Marriott School of Management at Brigham Young University (BYU), Utah, and asked a market research class to see if they could come up with new ways to market the product online. The student group presented their findings and said: '92% of the people who would actually like to try Orabrush will not buy Orabrush on the Internet. We suggest you drop the idea of marketing Orabrush on the Internet.' A student (Jeffrey Harmon) who was not a part of the project raised his hand and asked, 'That means 8% probably will buy Orabrush. That is millions of people, why don't you focus on them?' Dr. Bob approached Jeffrey after the class. He wanted to learn more about what Jeffrey had to say. Jeffrey said, 'I love your product. I could sell Orabrush online.' Dr Bob offered Jeffrey his old motorcycle (at 75 years old, Dr. Bob did not ride his motorcycle much anymore) in return for helping market Orabrush.

Jeffrey was thrilled and started working on Orabrush in the mornings and at nights before and after his full-time job. Jeffrey noticed a guy on a team he managed at his full-time job, Austin Craig. Austin had just graduated in Broadcast Journalism and was working as an intern. Jeffrey asked Austin, 'How much would I have to pay you to be in a video for me where you rant about bad breath?' Austin thought. 'A hundred bucks.' Jeffrey took his idea to his good friend, Joel Ackerman (a talented local script writer) and asked him if Joel could work some magic on this YouTube idea. As a favor for a friend, Joel quickly whipped out a clever script. Austin, Jeffrey, Dr. Bob, and Jeffrey's old roommate Devin Graham (a film major) shot the first Orabrush movie in a pool club. Dr. Bob held the microphone while Austin was acting, and Jeffrey did his best to direct his first video ever. In total, the video ('Bad Breath Test – How to Tell When Your Breath Stinks') cost Dr. Bob around $500. It introduced the Orabrush and was offering the product for purchase online. The video was a huge success, garnering nearly 27 million views (by the end of February 2017), and bringing Orabrush to the attention of end-users, major distributors and retailers. The quirky, commercial-style video explained that 90 percent of bad breath comes from bacteria on the tongue – hence the solution, the Orabrush tongue cleaner. The online price for the product package (one Orabrush and one tongue foam bottle) is $10.

After the explosive reaction to their first video, Harmon took on the role as chief marketing officer and began creating regular webisodes, introducing new characters like Morgan, a giant dirty tongue. Harmon then used YouTube video ads to reach more people and grow their fan base. The videos on the 'Cure Bad Breath' channel built a loyal following, and their YouTube channel since then grew to nearly 50 million views.

After two years, Orabrush had sold more than a million tongue cleaners to people in 40+ countries. The Orabrush brand became so popular that local pharmacy store managers began contacting Orabrush directly, citing requests from customers who had heard about the brand online. Because of the YouTube campaign, Walmart started to be interested in the product and late 2011 they began carrying the Orabrush tongue cleaners in its 3,500+ stores across the United States. And a few months later, CVS Pharmacy added the Orabrush tongue cleaner. CVS is the largest pharmacy chain in the United States with more than 7,400 stores.

Figure 4.20: Orabrush Website

Source: https://www.orabrush.com/; accessed 4th May 2020

Orabrush always had an innovative approach for mixing the new media.
For example, Orabrush created a Bad Breath Detector app for the iPhone.
The video (http://www.youtube.com/watch?v=SVvFD5JFnP4) promoting
the app has more than 1.9 million views and drove more than 300,000
downloads.

Then, in October 2012, Orabrush announced its latest product, the
Orapup, a novel tongue cleaner to help cure dogs' bad breath. The company also launched a campaign on the crowdfunding site Indiegogo.com in
an effort to bring the category-creating Orapup to market more quickly.

The company's goal was to raise $40,000. It raised $62,572 in the allotted
time period. In March 2015, Orabrush was acquired by one of its competitors, DenTek, which develops and markets oral care products, including
Floss Picks, Interdental Brushes, Disposable Picks, Tongue Cleaners and
Dental Guards. DenTek was founded in 1984 by John E. Jansheski.

DenTek is a leader in US retail sales of manual dental tools and accessories.

Source: Based on Hollensen (2015), pp. 541-543, adapted

In the following sections, we will summarize the most important aspects to consider when integrating YouTube in your marketing communication.

Create Channel Icon and Art

When you set up your own YouTube channel you first need to determine your **channel icon**. Think of your channel icon as your profile picture. You can either upload an image or choose a still image from one of your videos. If you upload an image (as we would recommend), consider the following specifications (Young, 2013):

- JPG, GIF, BMP, or PNG file (no animated GIFs)
- 800 x 800 px image (recommended)
- Square or round image that renders at 98 X 98 px

For your channel art, YouTube recommends that you upload a single 2560px by 1440px image. This provides the best results on all kinds of screens and devices, including desktops, laptops, phones, tablets, televisions, or any other place with pixels.

Create a Channel Trailer For New Viewers

You can have a video trailer show to all new visitors to your channel. Your channel trailer is like a movie trailer - use it as a way to offer a preview of your channel's offerings so viewers will want to subscribe. By default, ads will not appear when the trailer is playing on the channel page in the trailer spot (unless the video you have chosen contains third-party claimed content). This helps keep the user focused on learning about and subscribing to your channel. If the viewer is already subscribed to your channel, they will see a video under 'What to Watch Next' instead (Young, 2013).

Quick tips for creating channel trailers (Young, 2013):

- Assume the viewer has never heard of you.

- Keep it short.
- Hook your viewers in the first few seconds.
- Show, do not tell.
- Ask viewers to subscribe in your video and with annotations.

Figure 4.21: YouTube Channel of Marc Oliver Opresnik

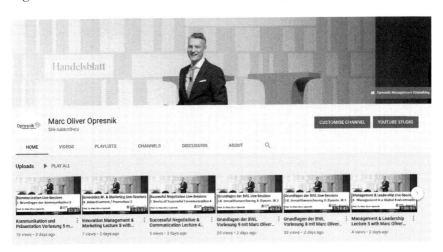

Source: https://www.youtube.com/c/OpresnikManagementConsulting/; accessed 4th May 2020

Managing Your Channel

Your channel is where you can organize your video content for your audience. As a channel owner, you can add videos, playlists, and information about yourself or your channel for visitors to explore (Agrawal, 2017; Young, 2013; Siu, 2016):

1. Sign in to your YouTube account.
2. On the left, select 'My channel'.
3. Use the drop-down menu next to your name to view your channel as 'Yourself', a 'New visitor', or a 'Returning subscriber'. When you

want to go back to viewing as yourself, click Done at the top of the screen.

4. Use the tabs to navigate previewing the channel:
   a. Home: This is what your audience sees when they visit your channel. They can view a feed of your activities or preview different sections of your customized layout.
   b. Videos: Use this to see a list of all uploads publicly available for subscribers or all of the videos you have publicly liked. You can sort by most popular or date added.
   c. Playlists: This is a list of all the playlists that you have created.
   d. Discussion: If you have turned on the discussion tab, this will display comments left on your channel.
   e. About: Use this to add a channel description (maximum length of 1,000 characters), set your channel country, enter a business contact email address, and define social or other web links. Links that you add here are featured just below your description and use the icon from the corresponding social network when displayed. You can overlay up to five of these links on your channel art as shortcut icons. To edit your 'About' tab, hover over the content, then click edit.

Tips to Improve Your YouTube Marketing Strategy

When it comes to marketing on YouTube, there is not only one golden rule you need to know. That being said, here are the most important things you can do to considerably improve your YouTube marketing strategy (Agrawal, 2017; Young, 2013; Siu, 2016):

- **Do your research**: One of the most undervalued aspects of content marketing is getting a firm grasp of the landscape. Before you start publishing your own content, you should take some time to look around at who else is playing in your market, and what they are doing to succeed.

- **Make a list of content buckets**: YouTube marketing really comes down to picking a few key areas where you feel you can deliver authentic thought leadership, entertainment, or some kind of value, and then mass producing content that falls within those larger buckets. For example: Say you are a soap company, and you want to use YouTube to sell more soap. Maybe one 'bucket' could be education - you want to educate people on why soap is important, for example to prevent themselves from getting sick. Another 'bucket' could be reviews - you want to review the best soaps on the market, and then direct people to where they can buy them. As soon as you start thinking this way, you will find it much easier to come up with not only quality content but content that always falls in line with your overall strategy.

- **Produce value-adding content and pique curiosity**: Studies have shown that viewers decide during the first 15 seconds of a video whether they are going to keep watching or not. Consequently, you should aim to build trust or curiosity within the first 15 seconds of your video. Users are not going to click on your video to see a boring infomercial. They may be willing to tolerate a dry tutorial if it offers unique advice that they will not find elsewhere. The most successful YouTube videos, though, tell an original and interesting story. It is easier to come up with great content ideas if you do not limit yourself to videos that relate directly to your product or business. This is particularly important if you are in an industry that is hard to get people excited about. Your goal is to keep viewers engaged long enough to soften them up for your call to action which is to visit the URL at the end of your video to learn more about your product or company. Make sure that your videos evoke the emotions you want customers to feel about your company, even if there is not a direct connection between your video content and the product you are ultimately promoting.

- **Support customer research with keywords**: When marketing on YouTube, it is important to recognize and consider your audience's stage in the buying process. Some marketers try to cold-sell to customers and prospects who might be interested in their products and services. The problem is that people who find your videos on YouTube are usually in the discovery stage and are not always ready to commit to a purchase. For this reason, it is important to choose keywords that are relevant to people who are looking for new information and to provide video content that educates based on those keywords. What types of keywords should you look for? Consider words and phrases that are relevant to both your industry and products and services. For example, if you have a car repair shop, you could target keywords such as 'how to change oil' and 'auto mechanic.'

- **Optimize your channel page to drive traffic**: Many advertisers focus exclusively on monetizing traffic to their video pages. While most viewers will find your video content first, they will also look at your YouTube channel page. Take advantage of those views to drive traffic to your other online properties. As stated above, you should manage your channel properly and optimize your channel page by providing relevant information about your company and including links to your website and other social media profiles. In addition, make good use of your banner header, where you can insert clickable links. Be sure to add appropriate calls to action there.

- **Create calls to action**: The key to any successful marketing campaign on YouTube is creating clear and concise calls to action. Depending on the message, you can use the beginning, middle, or end of a video to direct the actions of your viewers. Having too many prompts can cause confusion, so keep your CTAs minimal and simple. The goal is to make it as easy as possible for viewers to perform an action. Here are a few important actions to use on your videos:

    o   Subscribe: Give your viewer a reason to subscribe (e.g., new videos every week or never missing an episode).
    o   Like / Add to Favorites / Share: Ask your viewers to 'like' and 'share' the video so your content appears in more places across YouTube.
    o   Comments: Encourage your audience to participate by asking a specific question or requesting a topic they would like to see covered in an upcoming video.
    o   Video Graphics: Create a video 'end slate' that appears at the end of the video to direct viewers to your website.

- **Create regular content**: Consistently updating your channel with fresh content will keep your channel feed active, increase your presence on YouTube, and help you build an audience. Ideally, you should aim for a minimum of one video per week, but the right amount of content depends on your audience, your goals, and your content. One simple way to create a steady stream of content is to produce shorter versions of long-form content. Build a theme around a topic and then post bite-size versions of the theme on a weekly basis. This will keep your audience engaged and coming back for more.

- **Add sophisticated descriptions**: Pay attention to optimize the first 1-2 sentences in the description with a link back to your web-site or landing page. This is essential because YouTube truncates your description, and only the first 2 sentences are shown when viewers watch your video. You will also want to include relevant keywords here as already mentioned. Again, try to strike the fine balance of intriguing content that is also SEO friendly. Finally, you will want to end the description with URLs to other important sites, such as your social media presence, blog, website, etc.

- **Make use of tailored thumbnails**: Along with your video title, thumbnails act as mini marketing banners for your videos. If you have custom thumbnails enabled on your account, you should al-ways upload a custom thumbnail along with the video. The right thumbnail can attract a huge audience on YouTube. While you are filming your video, consider what your ideal thumbnail will be, so you can take certain shots or pictures while you are on location.

- **Collaborate with influencers**: One of the most effective ways to get your content disseminated, shared, and seen is by collaborating with other people who have audiences as well. The biggest YouTu-bers and successful brands are well known for effectively collabo-rating. It is a win-win for everyone involved. When you collaborate with someone else who has a similar audience as you, they get ex-posure to your audience and you get exposure to theirs. This is also an extremely viable alternative to buying viewership through ads, for example. Collaborations are far more organic, and if you do it right, you can collaborate with bigger and more well-known chan-nels to increase your own credibility. Many people are very open to collaborating. All you have to do is reach out with an idea, let them know what you would potentially need from them, and then go out and create it together.

YouTube Analytics

You cannot manage what you cannot measure. YouTube's analytics tool provides valuable data and insights about your content and audience. While YouTube provides a suite of information, we will touch base on three of the main sections – viewership, watch-time, and traffic source (Young, 2013; Siu, 2016):

- **Viewership**: YouTube gives you view counts for each video and channel. Analyze your most viewed days, weeks, and individual videos to understand why they are successful. You should also investigate the causes or catalysts for the high viewership and build on them. Was it the headline? Was there something in the news that caused the spike? In addition, take a look at the comments on the video to see if you can find useful information. Do not forget to make sure the successful videos are annotated to drive subscribers, comments, and traffic to your other videos.
- **Watch-time**: YouTube analytics also features data for viewer watch-time on your channel and on a per-video basis. While getting views is important, knowing how long your viewers are watching your videos is a much stronger indication or performance. Remember, YouTube is optimizing its search and discovery algorithm based primarily on watch-time, so it is a metric you must definitely pay attention to. Look for videos with the highest view-duration percentages and longest total watch-times. These are the videos that you should use annotations on to promote your channel or other videos.
- **Traffic source**: Traffic source helps you understand how viewers discover your content on a channel and per-video level. When examining individual video traffic, you can see which other specific videos are driving views via suggested or related video placement. Use these insights to optimize your metadata, thumbnails, and tags.

For your top-performing videos, analyze the first 1-2 weeks after they were published to discover what may have caused the spike.

4.3.6 Reddit

Founded in 2005, **Reddit** is a US-based social news aggregation, web content, and discussion website. Reddit is very different from other social media sites, like Facebook and Instagram. These emphasize more visual marketing, creating events and targeting groups. When it comes to Reddit marketing, a marketer has to use content, promote URLs and target a particular community. This site is not only well known to promote a brand, in fact, it can improve SEO activities which directly affects search engine rank. When brands are spending heavy amounts to boost up search engine ranks, small entrepreneurs can do it with Reddit without spending money or giving much effort. Reddit's registered community members can submit content, such as text posts or direct links. Registered users can then vote submissions up or down to organize the posts and determine their position on the site's pages. The submissions with the most positive votes appear on the front page or the top of a category. Content entries are organized by areas of interest called 'subreddits'. The subreddit topics include news, science, gaming, movies, music, books, fit-ness, food, and image-sharing, among many others (Aaron, 2013).

The unique feature of Reddit account is one can promote the links of their own content or post on other updates. Content is a key point for all type of online marketing strategy, hence in Reddit also the content is the main ingredient. If a content is fresh and unique, it will get more upvotes, backlinks, and text. The marketer can be asked for relevant URL for the content and through this improve in SEO ranks (Aaron, 2013).

Reddit has rapidly evolved over the years into one of the largest and most diverse places on the internet. Covering nearly every niche, redditors decide what types of content are popular. By using this crowd-sourced model, Reddit provides extraordinary content, ranging from informative and funny, to inspiring and helpful. With social power, comes great responsibility. Reddit has a reputation for weeding out poor content and making sure the good stuff gets publicity (most of the time). Gaining this publicity is not as simple as posting something on Facebook or Twitter, where you have already fostered a community. These five steps will help understand what 'redditing' actually is and how to do it well (Aaron, 2013).

Figure 4.22: Link promotion via Reddit

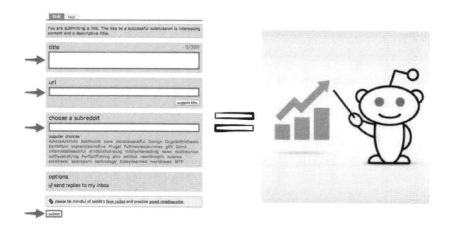

Source: https://bit.ly/3eXNtsu/; accessed 4th May 2020

Step 1: Observe and Take Notes

Those who are new to Reddit must understand the communal organization. Basically, content is divided into appropriate categories called 'subreddits' and every subreddit has unique rules that must be strictly followed. So, if we are in a subreddit called 'marketing' we first read through the right sidebar, learning this is a place for strictly articles and discussions. If we want to ask marketing-related questions or feedback, we must navigate to the subreddit 'AskMarketing'. We should also take note of the number of readers (subscribers) and users currently online (Aaron, 2013).

After digesting the rules, browse through top articles and sort by relevance + links from all time. This gives us a perfect idea of what types of content performs best. Take note of these, paying attention to any recurring themes and write down ways to provide similar content. Once these basics have been covered, do a search for your company name. If anything comes up, read through the results and record the most important findings.

Step 2: Adopt Social Norms

We start with understanding the framework of a subreddit, but now it's time to get social. Reddit comment sections are information gold mines. They're filled with opinions, suggestions, feedback, wishes, and complaints. It can be a heated place. Try to observe and try to adopt the social norms. Take note of how interactions start and end. Learn relevant acronyms, especially tl;dr (too long, didn't read). Certain subreddits, usually the smaller ones of some thousand readers, have fostered an incredibly helpful community. If we see regular users being resourceful and demonstrating professionalism and maturity, we know these are great outreach targets (Aaron, 2013).

Step 3: Plan Your Post

We have identified the subreddits most relevant to our industry and understood the rules, taken note of the most successful content, and become familiar with proper behaviour. Now we must create something based on everything we have absorbed. Develop a goal such as increasing conversion of product 'x' or increasing awareness of 'random service'. This process can be simple.

Step 4: Most Importantly, Engage Redditors

This step can be messy if we are not careful with our words. As previously mentioned, redditors will say whatever they want to say and most times we will not have our brand advocates to defend us. As the OP (original poster) we must continue the conversation (Aaron, 2013).

Depending on the subreddit, there are different modes of communication. For instance, we may be simply answering technical questions while other times we are facing critics. If we can answer difficult and sometimes 'loaded' questions with answers that demonstrate honesty and brand stability, redditors will usually up-vote in appreciation.

Step 5: Monitor and Measure Results

If our post is doing well, people are commenting, asking questions, and we are providing outstanding responses. It is time for the last time; monitoring and measuring.

This is where the measurement tools come into play: For example, we can use Google Analytics – Monitor views, clicks, demographics, etc. from the initial post to the moment the comment section has naturally finished (Aaron, 2013).

A 'failure' Reddit Marketing Case

Brands that try to insert themselves into memes are bound to fail. When Pilot posted an image of its G2 pen calling it the 'only pen that matters,' Redditors pushed back. As 'prosthetic4head' wrote: 'Even if he's not paid by the company or an advertising agency, I don't really want people who are just fans of some brand making accounts just to post about that product. What would reddit be then?'

A 'successful' Reddit marketing case

One of the best-in-class examples of a brand using Reddit was Nissan, which got two real community managers to ask people about the crazy things they could buy off Amazon, then actually went ahead and bought them.

Figure 4.23: Nissan successfully applying Reddit marketing

Source: https://bit.ly/2YaXZqn; accessed 4ᵗʰ May 2020

Then, a Redditor posted an image of an enormous Amazon box on a truck -- which happened to contain a Nissan Versa Note. The picture went viral. Nissan got good PR. Redditors got good content.

4.3.7 Blogging

The term **blog** is derived from the combination of 'web' and 'log' or 'weblog'. It originally began in the 1990s as an online diary. At that time, blogs were usually built websites that were updated and uploaded manually. It was not until the late 1990s, when platforms were created, that facilitated blogging without knowing coding or web design. In the early 2000s, **WordPress** appeared, and quickly grew into one of the most widely used blogging platforms (Zarella, 2010; Duermyer, 2016).

Nowadays, contemporary bog software provides a variety of social features, including comments, blogrolls, trackbacks, and subscriptions that make it perfect for marketing purposes. Blog make great hubs for your other social media marketing efforts, as they can be easily integrated with nearly every other tool and platform.

Blog Marketing and Benefits of Business Blogs

Blog marketing is the process of reaching your target market through a blog. Many companies use a blogging platform, such as WordPress, for both their site and blog (Duermyer, 2016). Nowadays, nearly every major company with a website has a blog that speaks to its current and potential customers. Like posts at other social media platforms, blogs should be conversational in tone. You can utilize blog marketing to inform and discuss with your audience developments that affect your industry such as the Internet of Things (IOT).

Against this background, every company with a website should have a blog that speaks to its current and potential customers as real people. Like posts at other social media platforms, blogs should be conversational in tone. You can utilize blog marketing to inform and discuss with your audience developments that affect your industry such as the Internet of Things (IOT). Blogging provides new content to customers and offers a way for consumers and businesses to interact.

Here are the most important benefits (Duermyer, 2016):

- **Inexpensive to start and maintain:** While there are free blogging platforms to run a professional appearance, it is advisable to make use of a self-hosted option in order to have a customized blog marketing for your enterprise.
- **Effective way to have new and return traffic come to your site:** Offering tips, updates and other new content gives users a reason to return to your business website.
- **Easy of use:** Most blogging platforms are quite easy to use via commands such as 'copy' and 'paste' and via functions such as 'drag and drop'.

- **Enhances search engine marketing:** Search engines such as Google like to find and rank fresh content, and many people blogg in particular in order to optimize their search engine ranking. Every time you write a blog, it is one more indexed page on your website, which means this is one more opportunity for you to show up in search engines and drive traffic to your website in organic search.

- **Allows you to demonstrate your expertise and gain trust:** The best business blogs answer common questions their customers have. If you are consistently creating content that is helpful for your target customers, it will help establish you as an authority in their eyes. With a blog you can demonstrate that you are an expert by providing insightful information which adds value.

- **Connect with your customers:** While most enterprises use Facebook and other social media platforms more than blogs to engage their consumers, blogs can allow you to have an in-depth conversation with your target customers. This allows you to build relationships, as well as get feedback and enhance customer service.

- **It can make money beyond your product or service:** You can allow advertising, promote affiliate products and get sponsors, adding additional sources of revenue and traffic.

- **It helps drive traffic to your website:** Blogging also helps you get discovered via social media platforms. Every time you write a blog post, you are creating content that people can share on social networks which helps expose your business to a new audience that may not know you yet.

How to Do Effective Blog Marketing

As we have highlighted above, blogging can help you improve your social media marketing substantially. In the following paragraphs, we will highlight the most important tips to enhance your social media efforts using blogging (Duermyer, 2016; Zarella, 2010; Kawasaki and Fitzpatrick, 2014; Scott, 2015):

- **Set up a blog marketing plan:** Setting a goal and specifying it in the form of a blog marketing plan helps ensuring your social media marketing manager follows a consistent process. You have to state what you are going to share on your blog such as news, tips, resources etc. Furthermore, you should specify, how often you will update your blog e. g. daily, weekly, etc.

- **Set up your blogging platform:** Decide on your blogging platform, and set it up, including customization that fits your business. Be sure to use the same logo on your blog as on your website to retain consistency. If you use a free blogging platform – which is not recommended for business blogging - have a domain name pointing to the blog so make it easier for consumers to get to your site.

- **At the start, quickly fill your blog with several posts:** Readers do not like to visit a blog with only one or two posts, so at the beginning add ten or more posts quickly, and then go to your regular post schedule as specified in your blog marketing plan.

- **Share your blog posts in your social status updates:** You may post links to your blog posts on your other social media platform profiles such as Facebook or Twitter. However, please keep in mind that most your updates are not self-promotional. Please ensure to give your followers something more valuable to read than a product or service sales page. Sharing your blog content on your social sites also helps you demonstrate your business's knowledge in your respective industry. This positions you as an informational leader. Becoming known as an authority in your business will ultimately boost your business's exposure and your revenue generation. If you want to get more engagement when you share your content, use different ways of posting your status updates, for example, on Facebook, post a photo to your wall and link to your content in the text of the post, since photo posts tend to get higher engagement than posts with just a link in them. Figure out what works best for your audience. When you mention specific people, products or services in your blog content, be sure to mention them again in your social updates when you share your post on the social media platforms. You can use @usernames in tweets and tag relevant people on Facebook and Google+. This increases the likelihood that these stakeholders will also share your content with their audience, potentially increasing your business's exposure with a new audience.

- **Make social sharing easy:** A great way to drive even more traffic to your blog posts is to allow your audience to share content for you in a convenient way. Why do you want visitors sharing your content? One of the best reasons is to gain social proof for the content your business publishes. You will also start to gain more readers and subscribers from followers of those who share your content. The best way to encourage others to share your content is to include social sharing buttons on your blog, preferably at the top and bottom of your blog posts. Plugins that can help you achieve this include Add This (multiple blogging platforms; http://www.addthis.com/), Share This (http://www.share-this.com/), and Sociable (WordPress self-hosted; https://word-press.org/plugins/sociable/). Another great way to encourage sharing is to ask visitors to share your content. Consider it a great call to action to add to all of your posts.

  In addition, you should also make a Pinterest post for every blog post. When people re-pin a Pinterest post, it appears in the public timeline again. Therefore, pins have a longer life, as they are 're-born' and drive more traffic to your blog post. Many people pin articles to remind themselves to read the articles later or to collect them for future reference. Make this easy by adding a link to your blog post with a call to action that says 'Pin it for later' and that points to the blog's pin.

  Finally, you should facilitate social log-in which enables people to sign in to your website or service by using their credentials from Twitter, Facebook, Plus and other platforms. This provides a faster and easier registration, integration of existing avatars, display of contact information, and reduction of spam as people are usually authenticated.

- **Make an effort to respond to as many -comments as you can:** Many blogs have a comment section below each post where users can leave comments. This section is a great place to build a strong community and get valuable feedback. Try to make it a commitment to respond to as many comments as you possible can, in particular when your blog is first starting out. If someone leaves a negative comment that is based – from his perspective – on some legitimate concern, respond to it, do not ever delete it to stay authentic. Since others are always watching, you should stay positive and pleasant. If you cannot stay positive, you can always 'agree to disagree' as this will fight of so-called 'trolls' – people who are always looking for a dispute and conflict. If everything fails, also do not hesitate to ignore, delete, block or report trolls and spammers. You do not have a moral obligation to engage with them, and there is little advantage to lowering yourself to that level.

Allow some time every day posting thoughtful comments on other blogs in your industry. Select a few well-known blogs that are relevant to your industry, and become a valuable member of their communities. This is an invaluable way to get connected to other people, but you will need to balance this with the time and resources you spend creating your individual quality content.

In addition, use 'mentions', not 'hashtags'. The purpose of a hashtag is to help people share a topic. This is different from a response. For example, when Mercedes introduces a new car, and you want to discuss it with other people, you should use #Mercedes. When you make a comment about Mercedes or to Mercedes and want to ensure that the company sees it, you should use @Mercedes.

- **Choose a topic for your blogs you can strongly influence or even dominate:** Focus on bringing your own voice and unique point of view forward and chose topics for our blogs and comments where you have an in-depth expertise and/or track record to demonstrate professionalism and add value.

- **Be responsive to news and blog fast:** The most popular kind of content you will be able to publish is breaking, exclusive news. The issue, of course, is that breaking news is difficult to come by. The best way is to establish connections with people working in your industry. In case you do hear about something you may blog about, act fast. There is little benefit to publishing second or third. Try to be responsive to breaking news and get as many details and as much media – such as photos, videos, or audio – as you can before you blog.

- **Maximize the impact of your blog:** Apart from breaking news and exclusive information you should also concentrate of blog contents that are likely to drive the most comments.

  One example includes lists as readers find content that is broken into short bits easier and more interesting to read. Rank the 10 best of a certain subject or the 10 worst. If possible, ass images and videos for each item and list them in descending order.

  Another potentially big lever to your blog impact can be tutorials so if you do know how to do something better than other people, make 'How-To's'. Add video or images, and break the steps down into a numbered list. The simpler you can make a seemingly complex task, the more your readers will appreciate your contribution. Useful information is one of the most commonly shared types of content on the Web, so blogs such as these are known to potentially spread fast.

  Another potential though dangerous lever is controversy. If you can disprove or make a strong case against something that the majority likes (or dislikes), you may have a huge number of comments and buzz. However, you have to be careful not to inflame tempers too much. Also, avoid making personal attacks, and always pay attention to stick to your facts.

- **Write guest posts:** Guest posts for websites such as 'HubSpot' (https://www.hubspot.com/), 'Huffington Post' (http://www.huffingtonpost.com/) or 'MarketingProfs' (https://www.marketingprofs.com/) can expose you to new audiences. They are a powerful option to grow your online exposure and visibility. Against this background, you should contact other websites and blogs that might be interested in your guest post. You will be surprised to learn than many are more than interested to get additional content.

- **Grow your social followers through your blogging:** Blogging gives you a platform and provides opportunities where you can encourage visitors to connect with you on social media platforms. Why do you want to build relevant followers through your blogging? These will be some of the best social followers for your business as they will be the most loyal ones and most interested in your industry and in your content. A relevant and targeted audience can ultimately turn into more leads and conversions for your business through social media. As you grow your targeted following on social media platforms, you can also expect to receive more engagement when you share your content on your social profiles.

If you want to grow your Twitter follower base, be sure to use the official Twitter retweet button. This allows you to add your @username to the tweet and encourages people to follow your Twitter account after they tweet your posts. Include a call to action at the end of your posts e. g. 'If you enjoyed this post, please follow us on Twitter and become a fan on Facebook.' This also helps increase your social following. Pay attention to only promote your main social media accounts as giving too many options may lead people to choose not to follow any of them. Since your business blog's design will likely feature a sidebar, include follow buttons so visitors can easily follow you on the top social networks.

- **Send social advertising links to your blog content:** If you find that the social advertising you have pointing directly to your landing pages, product pages and service pages is not getting enough substantial traffic, you may want to look at advertising links to your blog content instead. If your content is valuable enough and written toward your targeted customer base, you could generate conversions from the blog posts you advertise. If your goal is engagement, blog content characteristically gets more likes, comments and shares than sales pages. This will make your promoted posts on Facebook more impressive as Facebook ads can lead to boosting your number of fans on the platform. To create a great ad, start with a strong title, crisp description and image from your blog post. In addition, try making variations of your ad to test your audience's response and engagement using different images, titles and descriptions. To ensure that your ads are affecting your bottom line in a positive way, make sure to end each blog post with a strong call to action related to your products or services. This will give your ads more potential to lead to conversions and sales. Finally, analyze the data from each social network's advertising analytics, as well as your blog's Google Analytics, to make sure your ads are receiving click-throughs, and that your blog content is turning visitors into conversions.

4.3.8 TikTok

TikTok is a Chinese video-sharing social networking service owned by ByteDance, a Beijing-based company founded in 2012 by Chinese entrepreneur, Zhang Yiming. He has shown that a Chinese company, like ByteDance, can succeed in an openly competitive market internationally rather than only in China where the Great Firewall regulates the internet and blocks access to several U.S. social media sites. His strategy of dual versions of TikTok – one for China's internet censored market (Douyin) and another for the rest of the world (TikTok) – could be a new model for other digital content companies aiming for such global reach.

ByteDance first launched Douyin for the China market in September 2016. Later, TikTok was launched in 2017 for iOS and Android in markets outside of China. It became available in the United States after merging with musical.ly on August 2, 2018. TikTok and Douyin are similar to each other and essentially the same app, however they run on separate servers to comply with Chinese censorship restrictions.

The TikTok mobile app allows users to create a short video (dance, lip-sync, comedy, and talent videos) of themselves. To create a music video with the app, users can choose background music from a wide variety of music genres, edit with a filter and record a 15-second video with speed adjustments before uploading it to share with others on TikTok or other social platforms. They can also film short lip-sync videos to popular songs. As of March 2020, TikTok has 500 million active users per month. It has been made available in over 160 markets, and in 80 languages. TikTok users spend an average of 52 minutes a day on the app. ByteDance has stated that U.S. users open the app eight times a day and individual sessions on the app are the longest at 4.9 minutes (Fannin, 2019; Omar and Dequan, 2020). TikTok's geographical use has shown that approximately 40% of new users are from India. TikTok has proven to attract the younger generation, as approximately 40% of its users are between the ages of 16 and 24. Among these TikTok users, 90% say they use the app on a daily basis (Fannin, 2019). But, as all social media platforms do, TikTok will start to age up. So, we recommend evaluating whether to build a presence there. As TikTok added the ability to include links and commerce URLs in profiles and videos, you can also drive meaningful traffic to your website.

Exhibit 4.6

Chipotle's success story on TikTok

Chipotle is an American chain of fast casual restaurants specializing in tacos and burritos. In October 2019, Chipotle successfully launched a campaign to promote their $4 burritos on Halloween. In one post, digital magician and video star Zach King walks up to the counter at Chipotle to receive a burrito bowl with chips. After he pays, he jumps and his outfit changes in an instant into astronaut gear. Soon, everything in the store is floating in zero gravity.

Figure 4.24: Zach King's Chipotle TikTok video

Source: https://bit.ly/3eXTzt4; accessed 4th May 2020

Another star, Brittany Broski, posted on the video-sharing app around the same time, biting into a Chipotle burrito and then suddenly sporting a mad-scientist wig. All of these TikTok videos were tagged #boorito, for a U.S. advertising campaign which is one of the most viral campaigns ever on Tik-Tok based on one measure: the hashtag has 3.9 billion views on TikTok.

4.4 Social Entertainment Zone

Zone 3: Social Entertainment encompasses channels and vehicles that offer opportunities for play and entertainment. These include socially enabled console games, social games and gaming sites, and entertainment communities. MySpace used to be one of the largest social network companies in this category. From 2005 to 2009, MySpace was the largest social networking site in the world, and in June 2006 surpassed Google as the most visited website in the United States. Since then, the number of MySpace users has declined steadily despite several redesigns and it has lost its importance in the industry.

Another aspect of social entertainment is *entertainment communities*, which are still growing as a channel. It is anticipated that social entertainment communities will have a strong development around traditional areas of entertainment in the near future, including film, art, and sport.

4.4.1 eSports

Especially, **eSports** are experiencing high growth. ESports are a form of competition that is facilitated by electronic systems, particularly video games. Labelling video games as sports is a controversial point of debate, but the fact is that we see more and more professional teams. eSports tournaments are almost always physical events in which occur in front of a live audience. Among the most popular online streaming websites for such eSports tournaments is **Twitch**, which was acquired by Amazon in 2014. In 2017, eSports generated a worldwide turnover of 655 million US dollars, a significant increase of 493 million US dollars compared to the previous year. Revenues from eSports are expected to triple between 2018 and 2021 (to $1.65 billion), but even then they would only account for one percent of global sports revenues of over $150 billion. But eSports does reach tens of millions of people on a regular basis, and over a hundred million occasionally at some of the big events. As such, it is comparable to many traditional sports that have large audiences and big sponsors contracts. Consumers from the Asian markets made the largest contribution. They continue to lead the sector of the industry. Most of this input came from the countries

– Korea and China. League of Legends, which has been recorded as the top grossing PC game, has its top teams from Korea.

In Asia, top eSports players are major celebrities and gaming is a full-time job. In China, eSports is recognized by the General Administration of Sport, and plyers reside in gaming houses that are dedicated to training them. They have the best coaches, hand-eye co-ordination specialists, psychologists and agents at their disposal. South Korea has own dedicated eSports stadiums, and in this country eSports players attract audiences of millions and can attract massive prize pools from sponsors.

Apart from Dota 2 and League of Legends Counter-Strike is one of the most popular video games played among eSports teams. Here are teams playing as Terrorists or Counter Terrorists. The objective is to eliminate the enemy team over several rounds of play. The game consists of objectives such as planting the bomb (done by Terrorists) or defusing the bomb (Counter Terrorists) within a given amount of time.

4.4.2 Augmented Reality (AR)

Augmented Reality (AR) is where real-world environment whose elements are *augmented* (or supplemented) by computer-generated sensory input such as sound, video, graphics or GPS data. It is related to a more general concept called mediated reality, in which a view of reality is modified by a computer, tablet or a smartphone.

Thus, the technology functions by enhancing one's current perception of reality.

4.4.3 Pokémon Go

It seems that **Pokémon Go** will go down in history as the game that truly brought AR to the public at large. Here the players are required to interact with reality in order to play. Therefore, in Summer 2016 we were seeing millions of people running around parks and other pedestrian areas with their phones out 'looking for Pokémon'.

It is technology that interacts directly with real world environments and supplements them with new content. Pokémon Go accomplished this by making millions of people run around outside looking for cute little monsters that they could only see through their phone or tablet.

McDonald's was the first multinational to tie up with Pokémon Go for boosting sales in Japan. McDonald's was the first brand to advertise on Pokémon Go, paying to see 3,000 of its fast-food restaurants in Japan become 'Pokémon gyms' in the virtual reality game. Players must visit these locations to progress in the game by becoming the gym's champion. by hosting 3,000 of its outlets as 'gyms' for the game, or battle locations. Gyms are typically high-profile public places like train stations. The advantage for McDonald's is obvious: *Pokémon GO* players find themselves walking through the doors of McDonald's to do battle, and decide to buy a burger while they are there.

4.5 Social Commerce Zone
Zone 4: Social Commerce refers to the use of social media to assist in the online buying and selling of products and services. It is a subset of e-commerce, which is the practice of buying and selling products and services by the internet.

Exhibit 4.7

Amazon: Delighting Customers and Satisfying Customer Experiences Online

When you think about online shopping online, chances are good that you think first of Amazon.com. The online pioneer first opened its doors in 1995, selling books out of founder Jeff Bezos's garage in Seattle. Amazon still sells books but it now sells just about everything else as well, from music, electronics, tools, housewares, apparel, and groceries to fashions, loose diamonds, and Maine lobsters. Many marketers regard Amazon as the model for direct marketing in the digital age.

Amazon has grown impressively from the very beginning. Annual sales increased from 150 million dollars in 1997 to more than 157.16 billion dollars in 2017. Amazon is the youngest company in history to hit $100 billion in revenues (it took Walmart 34 years).

What has made Amazon such an amazing success story? Founder and CEO Bezos puts it into a nutshell by emphasizing that the company is obsessed over customers and that Amazon is relentlessly customer driven. He stresses that creating genuine value for customers is what drives everything. The overriding objective is to be the most customer-centric company in the world, where customers can find and discover anything they might want to purchase online. Amazon believes that if it does what it good for customers and satisfies their needs, profits will follow.

At Amazon, every decision is made with an eye toward improving the customer experience. In fact, at many Amazon meetings, the most influential figure in the room is 'the empty chair' which is literally an empty chair at the table that represents the all-important customer.

Perhaps more important than what Amazon sells is how it actually sells. The company wants to deliver a special experience to every customer. Amazon obsesses over making each customer's experience uniquely personal. For example, the Web site greets customers with their very own personalized home pages. In addition, its 'Recommendations for You' feature offers personalized product recommendations. Amazon was the first company to use 'collaborative filtering' technology, which sifts through each customer's past purchases and the purchasing patterns of customers with similar profiles to come up with personalized content.

Visitors to the Amazon site receive a blend of benefits: huge selection, good value, low prices, and convenience. But it is the 'discovery' factor that makes the buying experience special. Once on the Amazon site, users are compelled to stay for a while - looking, learning, and discovering. Amazon.com has become a kind of online community in which users can browse for products, research purchase alternatives, share opinions and reviews with other visitors, and chat online with authors and experts. In this way, the company does much more than just sell goods online. It creates and fosters direct, personalized customer relationships and satisfying online experiences. To create even greater selection and discovery for customers, Amazon has allowed competing retailers – from mom-and-pop operations to Marks & Spencer – to offer their products on Amazon, creating a virtual shopping mall of incredible proportions. Amazon even encourages users to sell used items on the site. The broader the selection attracts more customers, and everyone benefits. Year after year, Amazon places at or near the top of almost every customer satisfaction ranking, regardless of industry.

To date, Amazon has become the blue print for enterprises that are obsessively and successfully focused on delivering customer value online. Jeff Bezos has known from the very start that if Amazon creates superior value for customers, it will earn their business and loyalty, and success will follow in terms of profits and returns.

Source: Based on Kotler, Armstrong and Opresnik (2016), modified

Alibaba Group Holding Limited is another giant in the social commerce zone. It is a Chinese-American e-commerce company that provides consumer-to-consumer, business-to-consumer and business-to-business sales services via web sites. In addition, Alibaba provides electronic payment services, a shopping search engine and data-centric cloud computing services. The group began in 1999 when Jack Ma founded the website Alibaba.com, a business-to-business portal to connect Chinese manufacturers with buyers from overseas.

Social commerce uses social media applications to enable online shoppers to interact and collaborate during the shopping experience and to assist retailers during this process. Of course, just as in the physical world this may change the dynamics of shopping as it opens for others to influence our buying decisions. Social commerce channels include reviews and ratings of review sites or branded e-commerce sites (e.g. hotels.com, booking.com, Uber or Airbnb).

4.5.1 Uber

For example, for **Uber**, it is important to ensure a high-quality experience
At Uber, riders rate their experience at the end of every trip, and drivers do
the same. Uber regularly reviews that feedback and, through this process,
they can create and maintain a safe and respectful environment for riders
and drivers in more than 200 cities around the world. Rider feedback may
lead to deactivating a partner from the system or serve as validation that the
driver is providing great service. An Uber user is able to see a driver's rating
after the driver has accepted a ride request. That one- to five-star rating is
shown next to his or her photo, car type, and license plate number at the
bottom of the app.

4.5.2 Airbnb

Similarly, **Airbnb** is a community based on trust. Airbnb is an online marketplace and hospitality service, enabling people to list or rent short-term
lodging including apartment rentals, homestays, hostel beds, or hotel
rooms.

The origin of the name can be found in the founders' story: A combination
of 'Airbed' (the scrappy solution that Brian Chesky and Joe Gebbia had to
adopt in order to host their first guests) and 'Bed and Breakfast' (or BnB, a
way of hosting in which guests receive a warmer hospitality than hotels).

The company does not own any lodging; it is merely a broker and receives
percentage service fees (typically 15% commission of every booking from
guests and hosts – based on the total price paid) from both guests and hosts
in conjunction with every booking. It has over 3,000,000 lodging listings in
65,000 cities and 191 countries, and the cost of lodging is set by the host.
Like all hospitality services, Airbnb is a form of 'sharing economy'. One of
the key benefits of this 'home sharing' is to reduce costs for the travelers
and to help hosts earn some extra income. The price advantage for travelers
also means that Airbnb is increasingly competing with traditional hotel
groups. All the reviews on Airbnb are written by hosts and travelers from
the Airbnb community, so any review is based on a stay that a guest had in
a host's listing. The guest has 14 days after checkout to write a review for a

stay. Reviews are limited to 500 words and the guest can edit the review for up to 48 hours, or until the host completes his/her review.

4.5.3 Ratings and Reviews: Yelp

The most credible form of advertising comes straight from the people we know and trust. Eighty-three percent of online respondents in 60 countries say they trust the recommendations of friends and family, according to the Nielsen Global Trust in Advertising Report released in late September 2015. Moreover, sixty-six percent of survey respondents indicate that they trust consumer opinions posted online, which rates third in 2015 compared to TV ads (63%), ads in newspapers (60%) and magazines (58%).

User are already talking about your products, services, and brand online whether you are involved in the conversation or not. Consequently, it is instrumental to join the talks and have a presence on the appropriate review sites. Compared to other forms of online advertising, engaging review sites requires a lower investment of time and other resources, making it one of the most cost-effective things you can do. Many rating and review sites initially allowed users to post anonymously. Although not a classic review and rating site, Amazon.com, which was founded on July 5, 1994 by Jeff Bezos added user reviews already one year after its launch, giving everyone the power to anonymously review any product available on the site. Over time, most sites have incorporated a reputation system where users or their individual reviews can be rated on a scale of usefulness. More recently, a new kind of review sites has emerged that combines local rating with social networking features. The popular site Yelp.com, which was launched in 2004 and will be describes in more detail below, is an example of this type of site.

The next sections will introduce you to the common traits present across many review sites before we will deal in more detail with Yelp.com as the most popular one (Zarella, 2010):

- **Top Lists:** Review sites, in particular local ones, often have lists of the top businesses in certain categories (or neighborhoods).
- **Search:** The most usual way users find listings on review sites is with search. Rankings are typically a combination of relevance and

the number of highly acclaimed reviews. Due to this fact, it is important to include key words and phrases that people may use to search for a business like yours.

- **Responding:** Sites generally have a mechanism that allows you as the business owner to respond to reviews. Like stated in the section about blogging (cf. section 4.2.2) it is paramount to respond to as many comments as possible, also the positive ones. If a critical review makes you upset, do not respond right away but step away and keep calm. If a user has posted incorrect or misleading information, you should correct it accordingly but do not be offensive. Politely ask the reviewer if there is anything specific you can do to make the situation right, try to fix the problem if you can immediately, and eventually offer a discount to entice the user back to your business. As stated earlier, your response will be there for the entire Web to read, likely for a very long time s b sure it casts you and your business in a helpful light. Most negative reviews are the result of poor communication between a customer and an enterprise.

Yelp

Yelp is the largest local review directory on the Web. It enables people to search for local businesses based on customer ratings and reviews. It covers a broad range of industry sectors including food, beauty and spas, health and medical, home services, and many more. As a marketer, you can use Yelp to showcase your products and services, and connect with customers and prospects in your local area (Zarella, 2010).

Below is the key process as to using Yelp that, if understood and embraced, can turn the platform into a positive asset that helps your business (Zarella, 2010; Chaney, 2015; Patterson, 2016):

- **Claim Your Yelp Business Page:** Step one is to claim your respective Yelp business page. By doing so, you will be able to upload photos, add a link to your website, offer special and exclusive deals, respond to customer reviews, and ensure your business information is up to date. First, use the search function on the Yelp for business owners page (https://biz.yelp.com/) to find your company. Then, look for your listing on the drop-down menu that appears. When you find it, click the 'Claim this business' button. In the event your business is not listed, click the 'Add your business to Yelp' link and complete the form to add your listing. Fill out a form with your company name, email address, and password, and then click the 'Continue' button and run the authentication process of Yelp. Yelp uses a phone verification process to authenticate your business. Make sure you are near the phone you listed on the form. Your company phone will be called asking for the four-digit code that appears on the web page. Enter it into the telephone. Yelp will unlock your account giving you access to your business page (Chaney, 2015).

- **Check your business information:** Ensure your business information is accurate. That includes your business name, address, phone number, and hours of operation. Provide as much information as possible to aid people who may be searching for companies like yours. Having updated details also helps Google return correct information when people conduct searches that relate to your business category (Chaney, 2015).

- **Read and respond to customer reviews:** Reading reviews will help you better understand what customers think of your company, products and services. The more positive reviews you receive, the higher you will rank on Yelp. Consider negative reviews as feedback for how you can improve your processes and business. You can respond to customer reviews — both positive and negative — via a private message, or by posting a public comment that everyone can see. The private message function can be useful when responding to someone who has left a negative review. Public comments allow you to correct misinformation that may appear on a review or thank a customer for writing a positive review. Yelp does, of course, not allow you to remove or edit a negative review. It also asks that you not solicit reviews from customers (Zarella, 2010; Chaney, 2015; Patterson, 2016).

- **Post photos to your business page:** Photos are a useful way to showcase your business to prospective customers and add some visual interest to your page. For example, a hotel could post photos of its spa and other facilities such as restaurants and add favorite menu items or daily specials (Zarella, 2010; Chaney, 2015; Patterson, 2016; Kawasaki and Fitzpatrick, 2014).

- **Offer special deals:** Incentivize potential customers to visit your business with exclusive deals and gift certificates on your business page. 'Yelp Deals' are prepaid vouchers that offer consumers a discount at your place of business. When customers buy your deal or gift certificate, Yelp collects payment from the purchaser and retains a share of the purchase. The remainder is paid to you each month. Yelp keeps a record in the business page administrative console of all transactions by users who redeem the offers (Chaney, 2015).

- **Ask for recommendations:** You can ask your customers for reviews. When you know a customer is happy, you absolutely should ask them for a Yelp review (Chaney, 2015; Zarella, 2010).

- **Flagging does work, and you can ask for a re-review:** When a negative review comes in for a business, you should assess the content to see if anything violates Yelp's content guidelines. Not all reviews violate them, but if there is anything questionable, it is certainly worth a try. The guidelines are short and worth understanding well. If there is indeed a violation you should highlight it and let it be removed by Yelp (Patterson, 2016).

- **Use Website badges and stickers:** To encourage reviews of your business, you can post Yelp badges on your site, informing your visitors that you are on Yelp and directing them to your reviews. Businesses that gained a certain number of positive reviews get stickers from the platform that say 'People love us on Yelp'. In case you qualify for these stickers you should display these (Zarella, 2010; Chaney, 2015; Patterson, 2016; Kawasaki and Fitzpatrick, 2014)!

- **Elite Yelp Squad:** Yelp has created groups for its most active members, so-called Yelp Elite Squads. Elite-worthiness is based on several things, including well-written reviews, high quality tips, a detailed personal profile, an active voting and complimenting record, and a history of playing well with others. Members of the Elite Squad are designated by a colorful Elite badge on their account profile. Yelp organizes networking events at local venues for elite squad members through community managers. Hosting on of these events could be a powerful lever to your business. So, in case your business has some positive reviews you could contact the respective community manager and offer your location as potential venue. You can nominate yourself for the Yelp Elite Squad at any time (Zarella, 2010).

Figure 4.25: Example of a Yelp Business Page

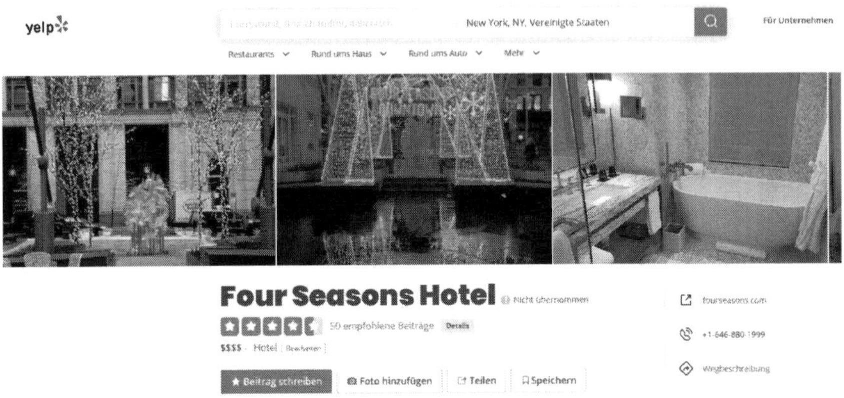

Source: https://bit.ly/2VHMp4t; accessed 4th May 2020

4.5.4 Expedia.com

In 1996, a small division within Microsoft launched an online travel booking site, **Expedia.com**, which became a pioneer in online travel booking. Expedia was spun off in 1999, and was later purchased by TicketMaster in 2001. Since then Expedia has evolved into the world's leading online travel company with a portfolio that includes some of the most well-known travel brands, including Trivago, Hotels.com and Travelocity. Expedia's revenue grew to US$ 10.06 billion in 2017.

In general, the online travel agency (OTA) industry has seen the development of various business models that have changed the way it has historically worked.

Basically, there are two different business models:

- **Merchant Model:** In this model, hotels sell rooms to OTAs in bulk at discounted or wholesale prices. The OTAs then sell them to customers at a markup price. This is the most commonly used model, and it benefits both parties.
- **Agency Model:** This is a commission-based model wherein hotels give OTAs commissions based on business bought. In this model, the hotels list their services, and the OTAs don't have to buy anything up front. This is beneficial for hotels, as it gives them the freedom to price their rooms, according to the actual demand development and the demand scenario, based on past sales.

Expedia uses both the merchant model and the agency model. Historically, the company has followed the merchant model, but with the agency model being more popular in countries like Europe, the Middle East, and Africa, the company has adopted it as well.

The company has an Expedia Traveler Preference program, which allows guests to decide how they would like to book each property, whether that is to pre-pay (as in the merchant model) or to pay at the hotel (as in the agency model).

The merchant model is generally more profitable for OTAs, as it normally provides higher profits, but also at a higher risk.

5. Social Media Marketing Controlling

5.1 Social Media Marketing Communication Objectives

Marketers are being overwhelmed with social media activities but there is little consensus on what one should be measuring. This section attempts to bring clarity to the situation by viewing social media metrics from the lens of integrated marketing communications.

Marketing communication metrics are necessary for the development and evaluation of marketing programs. In social media marketing, there are special challenges in choosing the right marketing metrics.

At the core of an integrated marketing communications program are the communication objectives, which in social media marketing can be (Barger and Labrecque, 2013):

- **Creating awareness:** one of the primary functions of social media is content sharing. When a message is shared widely within a relatively short period of time, it has gone viral and this leads to a rapid increase in awareness of both the message and the message's creator

- **Gaining consideration:** Consumers are increasingly turning to social media for product and service recommendations. This can have implications for monitoring social media for problems that a company's products or services can solve.

- **Stimulating trial:** Typically, sales promotions are used to stimulate trial of products and services. Common forms of online sales promotion include printable coupons, discount codes, contests and games.

- **Encouraging repurchase:** This method tries to retain existing customers and encourage repurchase through incentive schemes, which are focused on persuading customers not to switch to competitors. For example, companies can give a discount on a repurchase of the same product. Another method is the issue of 'stamps' that accumulated on a personal web account could be exchanged for another good or service. For example, Hotels.com provides their customers a free hotel room for every 10 hotel rooms they book through them.

- **Improving customer satisfaction:** The company can enhance the customer satisfaction by providing product and service support via social media. For example, software developers often receive and reply to requests for technical support on Facebook or Twitter. When it comes to dissatisfaction, customers can contact the company directly via social media. If the company deals with such complaints promptly and effectively, dissatisfied customers will be less likely to communicate their dissatisfaction to others. Furthermore, by monitoring social media for posts from recent customers, companies can reassure these customers that they made a good choice and thereby reduce their cognitive dissonance.

- **Building brand relationship:** Brand relationships develop because of positive repeat interactions between brand and customer. Companies can stimulate interaction with customers through posting relevant content, like news, articles, photos, videos and games.

- **Building brand communities:** Here the customers not only interact with the brand but also with one another through e.g. discussion forums. Brand communities may be organized by the company, that owns the brand, or it may be formed autonomously. Brand communities can serve as a resource for idea generation (e.g. through crowdsourcing) and marketing research.

The following tries to identify the social media metrics that are most informative to the marketer, in relation to achieving above communication objectives. The list of metrics differentiates between **non-financial** and **financial metrics**. Some of the most important social media metrics will be examined further in the following sections (Mintz and Currim, 2013; Barger and Labrecque, 2013).

5.2 Non-financial Social Metrics
Non-financial metrics attitudinal and behavioral measures. For example, the advertising 'hierarchy of effects' model (awareness, knowledge, liking

preference, conviction and purchase) is an attitudinal approach, whereas behavioral measures are more based on actions.

The most important metrics of this category are explained below.

Volume of Mentions

This is the count of total number of the brand's mentions in social media channels over a period of time. This simple metric can be a good indicator of 'awareness'.

The mentions can be classified by the tone of each mention: positive, neutral or negative.

Share of Voice (SoV)

Since negative mentions are typically not viewed as a competitive advantage, SoV is most of the calculated using positive mentions only, like this definition:

SoV (%) = Positive volume of brand / Positive volume of all brands in the category x 100

SoV is often benchmarked with the competition to provide an indication of how effectively a company is creating positive buzz.

Engagement

This term refers to the potential customers that take some action beyond viewing or reading a website. The 'engagement' is measured by these activities: 'liking' a brand's post, commenting on or replying to a brand's post, or sharing a brand's post with others.

Consequently, we use the following definition for the general term:

Engagement (%) = Number of engagement activities at time t with all posts to date / number of views at time t of all posts to date x 100

As 'the number of views' per post can be difficult to measure, some use the 'number of followers' as a rough approximation.

Advocates

Being 'engaged' is a necessary condition for reaching the final stage of brand commitment: Being a 'Advocate' for the brand, by creating and uploading content that actively promotes the brand, e.g. by posting a Facebook status update that recommends or speaks favorable of a brand.

Therefore, we use the following definition:

Advocates = Total number of social media participants who actively write positive posts about a brand during a specified period of time

This metric is especially important when a company's objective is to gain consideration and stimulate trial. Family and friends of advocates are more likely to consider a brand when an advocate speaks positively about it.

The following other 'operational' non-financial social metrics are more related to specific websites actions, but they are still extremely important to monitor.

Click-through Rate (CTR)

The purpose of the click-through rate metric is to capture customer initial response to websites.

The CTR for an advertisement is then defined as the number of clicks of an ad divided by the number of times the ad is shown:

Click-Through Rate (%) = Number of clicks of an ad / Number of times the ad is shown x 100

CTRs for banner ads has fallen over time. When banner ads were introduced, it was not uncommon to have rates above five per cent. Since then, these rates have fallen, currently averaging close to 0.2 or 0.3 per cent. The CTR often represents the top level of the conversion funnel, where the customer is navigating through a website and finally converting to a purchase (a sale).

Conversion Rate

This metric is used to describe the act of converging website visitors into paying customers. Sometimes 'conversion' is considered to be some sort of result other than a sale. However, here the term is defined as:

Conversion rate (%): Number of customers making an actual purchase / number of website visitors x 100

In this way, the conversion rate is measuring the relation between the top level (number of website visitors) and the bottom level (actual sale) of the conversion funnel:

- Improving the conversion rate is a long-term investment. It involves activities like:
- Improving website flow
- Improving customer online services
- Improving online customer satisfaction and experience

5.3 Financial Social Metrics

Financial measures emphasize the revenue generated by marketing communication activities.

Return on Investment (ROI):

In this context, ROI is mostly used to evaluate short-term social media objective, such as creating brand awareness, stimulating trial and encouraging repurchase. For example, a company may offer a printable coupon or communicate a discount code as part of their online campaign to stimulate trial among potential customers. Here ROI is defined as follows:

Return on Investment (ROI): (Extra revenue gained from campaign) – (Cost of campaign) / Cost of campaign x 100

Attributing extra revenues only to social media is of course a bit problematic, especially for online campaigns that do not offer an incentive. Even with campaigns that do offer an incentive, the calculation ROI ignores potential synergies between incentive-based and non-incentive-based campaigns.

Consequently, an alternative for the traditional ROI could be to consider return of investment from the customer's perspective; namely, what the customer gets for investing his or her time in engaging with a brand through social media.

Other metrics are more related to specific websites actions, but they are still extremely important to monitor.

Cost-per-Click (CPC) - (or Pay-per Click)

The cost-per-click metric is used to assess the cost effectiveness and profitability of online marketing.

It is a way to measure awareness and interest among potential customers.

Cost-per-Click = Advertising cost / number of times that the ad is clicked

There are two primary models for determining CPC:

- **Flat-rate:** Here the company and the website owner agree on a fixed amount that will be paid for each click. Of course, in many cases companies (advertisers) can lower rates (prices), especially when committing to a long-term or high-value contract.
- **Bid-based:** here the company (advertiser) signs a contract that allows it to compete against other advertisers in a private auction hosted by the website owner. Each company informs the host about the maximum price that he or she is willing to pay for a given ad spot of a website. The website owner then chooses the winning bidder with the highest price.

Conclusion

Web 1.0 provided easy access to information, entertainment, and communication tools. Web 2.0 fundamentally changed the consumers' role to being active providers in delivery of information (e.g. through YouTube). Through engaging in an ongoing dialogue with other persons and with companies, consumers' stake in the process increases. This results in more satisfying outcomes for producers and consumers. In web 2.0 each additional user adds value for all users, which is referred to as a network effect.

In order to plan social media marketing strategy that will meet objectives, marketers need to understand how their consumers are searching and interacting with others on the internet, to make their right buying decisions. Marketers' decisions are based on what we know about the target audience. In this context gathering market insight and competitive intelligence are critical steps in developing the right social media marketing strategy. Marketers rely on several variants of marketing research to make these decisions. In this context, social media research can include both secondary and primary research. As consumers participate in the social media zones (see below) they leave their digital social footprints, so their buying decision processes can be followed digitally until the final online buying decision.

All social media are networked around relationships, technologically enabled, and based on the principles of shared participation. We divided the Social Media into four zones where there are some overlapping:

- **Zone 1: Social Community** include channels of social media which are focused on relationships and the common activities people participate in with others who share the same interest. Thus, social communities feature two-way and multi-way communication, conversation, collaboration, and the sharing of experiences and resources. All social media channels are built around networked relationships, but for social communities the interaction and collaboration for relationship building and maintenance are the primary reason people engage in these activities. All the channels emphasize individual contributions in the context of a community, communication and conversation, and collaboration.
- **Zone 2: Social Publishing** sites aid in the dissemination of content to an audience. The channels of social publishing include

blogs, micro-sharing sites, media sharing sites, social bookmarking and news sites.

- **Zone 3: Social Entertainment** encompasses channels that offer opportunities for play and enjoyment. These include social games and gaming sites (e.g. within e-Sports), socially enabled console games, virtual worlds, and entertainment communities. At this stage in the development of social media, social games and gaming sites are by a substantial margin the most advanced channel in the social entertainment zone. Yet another aspect of social entertainment is entertainment communities. Social entertainment communities will develop around other traditional areas of entertainment in the near future - film, art, and sport.

- **Zone 4: Social Commerce** refers to the use of social media to assist in the online buying and selling of products and services. Social commerce leverages social shopping behaviors when online shoppers interact and collaborate during the shopping experience.

References

Aaker, D. A. (1990) Brand extensions: The good, the Bad and the Ugly, Sloan Management Review, Summer, pp- 47-56

Aaker, D. A. (1991) Managing Brand Equity, The Free Press, New York, NY

Aaker, D. A. (1996) 'Measuring brand equity across products and markets', California Management Review, vol. 38, no. 3, pp. 102-20

Aaron, J. (2013) 'How to incorporate Reddit into your Marketing Strategy in 5 easy steps, https://www.inboundnow.com/how-to-incorporate-reddit-into-your-marketing-strategy-in-5-easy-steps/, accessed 24th February 2017

Adcock, A. (2000) Marketing strategies for competitive advantage, Wiley

Agrawal, AJ (2017) 5 Tips To Improve Your YouTube Marketing Strategy, https://www.forbes.com/sites/ajagrawal/2017/01/12/5-tips-to-improve-your-youtube-marketing-strategy/#3210aac3494f, accessed 7th March 2017

ANA (2018), Survey Report – How ANA members are using influencer marketing, Association of National Advertisers, New York

Anderson, J. C. and Narus, J. A. (2004) Business Market Management: Understanding, Creating and Delivering Value, Prentice Hall, New Jersey

Andreasen, A. R. (1994) Social marketing: Its definition and domain. Journal of Public Policy and Marketing 13 (1), pp. 108-14.

Ansoff, H. I. (1965) Corporate Strategy: An Analytical Approach to Business Policy for Growth and Expansion, McGraw-Hill, New York

Bagozzi, R. P. (1974) Marketing as an Organized Behavioural System of Exchanges, Journal of Marketing, Vol. 38, October, pp. 77-81

Bainbridge, J. (2005) Third Dimension, Marketing, 8, June, p. 36

Baker, M. and Hart, S. (1999) Product Strategy and Management, Pearson: Education, Prentice Hall

Barger, V.A. and Labrecque, L.I. (2013) An Integrated Marketing Communications Perspective on Social Media Metrics. International Journal of Integrated Marketing Communications, Spring, pp. 64-76

Barnes, J. G. (1994) Close to the Customer: but is it really a relationship?, Journal of Marketing Management, 10, pp. 561-570

Barnes, J. G. and Howlett, D. M. (1998) Predictors of equity in relationships between service providers and retail customers, International Journal of Bank Marketing, 16 (1), pp. 5-23

Bartlett, C. and Ghoshal, S. (1989) Managing Across Borders: The transnational solution, Harvard University Press, Boston, MA.

Berman, B. (2016) Planning and implementing effective mobile marketing programs, Business Horizons, Vol. 59, July–August 2016, pp. 431–439

Berry, L. L. (1983) Relationship Marketing, in Berry, L.L., Shostack, G.L., Upah, G.D. (Eds.) Emerging Perspectives on Service Marketing, Chicago, IL: American Marketing Association, pp. 25-28

Berry, L. L. (1995) Relationship Marketing of Services Growing Interest, Emerging Perspectives, Journal of the Academy of Marketing Science, 23 (Fall), pp. 236-45

Berry, L. L. (2000) Relationship Marketing of services: growing interest, emerging perspectives, in Shet, J. N. and Parvakiyar, A. (eds) Handbook of Relationship Marketing, Thousand Oaks, pp. 149-170

Best, R. J. (2000) Market-Based Management, 2nd edition, prentice Hall, Inc

Bitner, M. J. (1995) Building Service Relationships: It's All about Promises, Journal of the Academy of Marketing Science, 23 (Fall), pp. 246-51

Brennan, R. (1997) Buyer/supplier partnering in British industry: the automotive and telecommunications sectors, Journal of Marketing Management, 13 (8), pp. 758-776

Brodie, R. J., Coviello, N. E., Brookes, R. W. and Little, V. (1997) Towards a paradigm shift in marketing: an examination of current marketing practices, Journal of Marketing Management, 13 (5), pp. 367-382

Bulygo, Z (2010) Facebook Marketing: A Comprehensive Guide for Beginners, https://blog.kissmetrics.com/facebook-marketing/, accessed 27th February 2017

Buttle, F. B. (1996) Relationship Marketing: Theory and Practice, Paul Chapman, London

Cannie, J. K., and Caplin, D. (1991) Keeping Customers for Life. American Management Association, New York.

Carlzon, J. (1985) Moments Of Truth, Albert Bonniers Förlag Ab, Stockholm

Carroll, A. B. and Buchholtz, A. K. (2000) Business and society: ethics and stakeholder management, South-Western College, Cincinnati

Chandy, R. K. and Tellis, G. J. (1998) Organizing for Radical Product Innovation, MSI Report, No. 98-102

Chaney, P. (2015) How to Use Yelp for Local Marketing, http://www.practicalecommerce.com/articles/114853-how-to-use-yelp-for-local-marketing, accessed 27t February 217

Charter, M. K., Peattie, K., Ottman, J. and Polonsky, M. J. (2002) Marketing and Sustainability, BRASS, Cardiff

Chartered Institute of Marketing (2005) Marketing and the 7Ps, Cookham, Chartered Institute of Marketing

Chaston, I. (1998) Evolving 'new marketing' philosophies by merging existing concepts: application of process within small high-technology firms, Journal of Marketing Management, 14, pp. 273-291

Christopher, M., Payne, A. and Ballantyne, D. (1991) Relationship Marketing, Butterworth Heinemann, London

Churchill, H. L. (1942) How to Measure Brand Loyalty, Advertising and Selling. Vol. 35, pp. 24ff

Collins, J. and Porras, J. I. (2002) Built to last – Successful habits of visionary companies, HarperCollins, New York

Crie, D. and Micheaux, A. (2006) From Customer Data to value: What is lacking in the information chain, The Journal of Database Marketing & Customer Strategy Management, 13 (4), 282-299

Croft, M. (2003) Mind your language, Marketing, June 19, pp. 48-49

Crosby, L. A. and Stephens, N. (1987) Effects of Relationship Marketing on Satisfaction, Retention, and Prices in the Life Insurance Industry, Journal of Marketing Research. Vol. 24, November, pp. 404-411

Daley, R. (2015) The Ultimate Pinterest Marketing Guide: How to Improve Your Reach and Promote Your Brand, https://blog.kissmetrics.com/ultimate-pinterest-marketing-guide/, accessed 15th February 2017

D'Andrea, M. (2012) The Marketer's Guide To SlideShare, https://blog.kissmetrics.com/marketers-guide-to-slideshare/, accessed 17th February 2017

Daneshkhu, S. (2014) 'Make-up enters age of selfie', Financial Times Europe, 29th July, p. 8

Davenport, H. (2001) How do they know their customers so well?, MIT Sloan Management Review, Winter, pp. 63-73

Davis, S. (2000) Brand asset management: Driving profitable growth through your brands, Jossey-Bass, San Francisco

Day, G. S. (2002) Managing the market learning process, Journal of Business & Industrial Marketing, 17 (4), pp. 240-252

Deloitte (2016), e-Sports: Bigger and smaller than you think, Deloitte Global www2.deloitte.com/global/en/pages/technology-media-and-telecommunications/articles/tmt-pred16-media-esports-bigger-smaller-than-you-think.html

DeMers, J. (2014): Your Guide To Using Snapchat For Marketing, http://www.forbes.com/sites/jaysondemers/2014/08/04/your-guide-to-using-snapchat-for-marketing/#635635c60f82

Dewsnap, B. and Jobber, D. (2002) A social psychological model of relations between marketing and sales, European Journal of Marketing, 36(7/8), pp. 874-894

Dibb, S. (2002) 'Marketing Planning best practices', The Marketing Review, No. 2, pp. 441-59

Dibb, S. and Simkin, L. (2001) Market Segmentation – Diagnosing and Treating the Barriers. Industrial Marketing Management, 30, 609-625

Douglas, S. P. and Craig, C. S. (2006) Collaborative and iterative translation: an alternative approach to back translation, Journal of International Marketing, 15(1): 30–43.

Doyle, P. (1989) Building successful brands: The strategic options, Journal of Marketing Management, 5(1), pp. 77-95

Doyle, P. (1995) Marketing in the new millennium, European Journal of Marketing, 29 (12), pp. 23-41

Drucker, P. F. (1993) Management Tasks, Responsibilities, Practices, Harper and Row, New York

Dube, A. and Helkkula, A., (2015) Service experiences beyond the direct use: indirect customer use experiences of smartphone apps", Journal of Service Management, Vol. 26 Iss 2 pp. 224 - 248

Duermyer, R. (2016) Blog Marketing: What It Is and How to Do It, https://www.thebalance.com/blog-marketing-1794404, accessed 20th February 2017

Dwyer, F. R., Schurr, P. H. and Oh, S. (1987) Developing buyer-seller relationships, Journal of Marketing, 51, pp. 11-27

Edelman, D.C. and Singer, M. (2015) 'Competing on Customer Journey', Harvard Business Review, 93(11), pp. 88-100

Egan, J. (2008) Relationship Marketing, Pearson Education, Harlow

Ehrenberg, A. S. C. (1992) Comments on how advertisement works, Marketing and Research Today, August, pp. 167-169

Ehrenberg, A. S. C. and Goodhart, G. J. (1980) How advertising works, J. Walter Thompson/MRCA

Emiliani, M. L. (2000) 'Business-to-Business online auctions. Key issues for purchasing process improvement'. Supply Chain Management: An International Journal. Vol. 5, No. 4, pp. 176-186

Evans, P. B. and Wurster, T. S. (1999) 'Getting Real About Virtual Commerce', Harvard Business Review, Vol. 77, No. 6, (November-December), pp. 85-94

Evans, P. B. and Wurster, T. S. (2000) Blown to Bits: How the new economics of information transforms strategy, Boston, Harvard Business School Press

Fanning, J. (1999) Tell me a story: The future of branding. Irish Marketing Review, vol. 12, no. 2, pp. 3-15

Fannin, R. (2019). The Strategy Behind TikTok's Global Rise. Harvard Business Review Digital Articles, 2–5

Faris, P. W., Bendle, N. T., Pfeifer, P. E. and Reibstein, D. J. (2006) Key Marketing Metrics, Pearson, Harlow

Fletcher, R., Bell, J. and McNaughton, R. (2004) International e-Business Marketing, Thomson Learning

Fontein, D. (2016) Pinterest for Business: The Definitive Marketing Guide, https://blog.hootsuite.com/how-to-use-pinterest-for-business/, accessed 15th February 2017

Francis, T. (2000) Divine Intervention, Marketing Business, May, pp. 20-22

Frazier, G. L., Spekman, R. E., and O'Neal, C.R. (1988) Just-In-Time Exchange Relationships in Industrial Markets, Journal of Marketing, Vol. 52, October, pp. 52-67

Gilmore, A., Carsons, D. and Grant, K. (2001) SME Marketing In Practice, Marketing Intelligence & Planning, 19 (1), Pp. 6-11

Go, G. (2016) Steps to Successful Forum Marketing, https://www.the-balance.com/successful-forum-marketing-2531792, accessed 17th February 2017

Gobe, M. (2001) Emotional branding, Allworth Press, New York

Gordon, I. H. (1998) Relationship Marketing, Etobicoke, John Wiley & Sons

Gotter, A. (2016) A Step-by-Step Guide to Pinterest Marketing, https://adespresso.com/academy/blog/step-step-guide-pinterest-marketing/, accessed 15th February 2017

Griffin, T. (1993) International Marketing Communications, Butterworth Heinemann, Oxford

Grönroos, C. (1990) Relationship approach to the marketing function in service contexts: the marketing and organization behaviour interface, Journal of Business Research, 20, pp. 3-11

Grönroos, C. (1994) From marketing mix to relationship marketing: towards a paradigm shift in marketing, Management Decisions, 32, pp. 4-20

Grönroos, C. (1995) Relationship marketing: the strategy continuum, Journal of Marketing Science, 23 (4), pp. 252-254

Grossmann, R. P. (1998) Developing and managing effective customer relationships, Journal of Product and Brand Management, 7 (1), pp. 27-40

Grossnickle, J. and Raskin, O. (2001) What's ahead on the Internet: new tools, sampling methods, and applications help simplify Web research, Market Research, Summer: 9–13

Habibi, M.R., Davidson, A. and Michel Laroche (2017) 'What managers should know about the sharing economy', Business Horizons, Vol 60, January-February, pp. 113—121

Haenlein, M. and Libai, B. (2018) Seeding, referral and Recommendation: Creating Profitable Word-of-Mouth Programs, California Management Review, 59(2), 68-91

Hall, E. T. (1976) Beyond culture, Garden City, NY: Anchor

Harridge-March, S. and Qinton, S. (2009): Virtual snakes and ladders: social networks and the relationship marketing loyalty ladder, The Marketing Review, 2009, Vol 9, No. 2, pp. 171-181

Hart, S., Smith, A., Sparks, L. and Tzokas, N. (1999): Are loyalty schemes a manifestation of relationship marketing, Journal of Marketing Management, 15, pp. 541-562

Hastings, G. (2003) 'Relational Paradigms in Social Marketing', Journal of Macromarketing, Vol. 23, No. 1, June pp. 6-15.

Hennig-Thurau, T. and Klee, A. (1997) The Impact of Customer Satisfaction and Relationship Quality on Customer Retention—A Critical Reassessment and Model Development, Psychology & Marketing, 14 (December), pp. 737-65

Hennig-Thurau, T., Hofacker, C.F. and Bloching, B. (2013) 'Marketing the Pinball Way: Understanding how Social Media change the generation of value for consumers and companies', Journal of Interactive Marketing, Issue 4, pp. 237-241

Hines, K. (2013) How to Improve Your Social Media Marketing With Blogging, http://www.socialmediaexaminer.com/how-to-improve-your-social-media-marketing-with-blogging/, accessed 20th February 2017

Hite, R. E. and Frazer, C. (1988) 'International advertising strategies of multinational corporations', Journal of Advertising Research, vol. 28, August - September, pp. 9-17

Hofacker, C.F., Ruyter, K.D., Lurie, N.H., Manchanda, P. and Donaldson, J. (2016), Gamification and Mobile Marketing Effectiveness, Journal of Interactive Marketing, Vol. 34, pp. 25–36

Hollensen, S. (2003) Marketing Management, Financial Times/Prentice Hall, London

Hollensen, S. (2006) Marketing Planning: A global perspective, McGraw-Hill, Berkshire

Hollensen, S. (2017) Global Marketing, 7th ed., Pearson Education Limited, Harlow, UK

Hollensen, S. (2015) Marketing Management, 3rd edition, Pearson Education Limited, Harlow, UK

Hollensen, S. (2014) Global Marketing, 6th ed., Pearson Education, Harlow, UK

Hollensen, S. (2019) Marketing Management – A Relationship Approach, 4th ed., Pearson Benelux, Amsterdam

Hollensen, S. and Opresnik, M. (2015) Marketing – A Relationship Perspective, 2nd ed., Vahlen, München

Hooley, G., Saunders, J. and Piercy, N. (2004) Marketing strategy and competitive positioning, 3rd ed., Financial Times/Prentice Hall

Houston, F. S., Gassenheimer, J.B., and Maskulka, J. (1992) Marketing Exchange Transactions and Relationships. Quorum Books, Westport, CT.

Howard, J. A., and Sheth, J. N. (1969) The Theory of Buyer Behaviour. John Wiley & Sons, Inc., New York

Ilieva, J., Baron, S. and Healey, N.M. (2002) Online surveys in marketing research: pros and cons, International Journal of Market Research, 44(3): 361–76.

Jain, S. (1996) International Marketing Management (5th ed), South-Western College Publishing, Cincinnati, OH

Javalgi, R. and Moberg, C. (1997) Service loyalty: implications for service providers, Journal of Services Marketing, 11 (3), pp. 165-179

Jaworski, B., Kohli, A. and Sahay, A. (2000) Market-Driven Versus Driving Markets, Journal of Academy of Marketing Science, 28 (1), pp. 45-54

Johnston, A. (2016) How to Create an Instagram Marketing Strategy, http://sproutsocial.com/insights/instagram-marketing-strategy-guide/, accessed 14th February 2017

Jones, J. P. (1991) Over-promise and under-delivery, Marketing and Research Today, November, pp. 195-203

Jones, T. O. and Sasser, W. E. (1995) Why satisfied customers defect, Harvard Business Review, November/December, pp. 88-99

Kandampully, J. and Duddy, R. (1999) Relationship marketing: a concept beyond the primary relationship, Marketing Intelligence and Planning, 17 (7), pp. 315-323

Kanter, R. M. (1994) Collaborative advantage, Harvard Business Review, July/August, pp. 96-108

Kawasaki, G. and Fitzpatrick, P. (2014) The art of social media, Random House.

Keegan, W. J. (2002) Global Marketing Management, 7th ed., Prentice-Hall, Upper Saddle River, New Jersey

Keller, K. L. (1993) 'Conceptualizing, measuring, and managing customer-based brand equity', Journal of Marketing, vol. 57, no. 1, pp. 1-22

Kinard, B. R. and Capella, M. L. (2006) Relationship Marketing: the influence of consumer involvement on perceived service benefits, Journal of Service Marketing, 21 (6), pp. 359-368

Klompmaker, J. E., Rodgers, W. H. and Nygren, A. E. (2003) 'Value, not volume', Marketing Management, June, pp. 45-48

Kohli, A. K. and Jaworski, B. J. (1990) Market orientation: the construct, research propositions and managerial implications, Journal of Marketing, 54, pp. 1-18

Kohli, C., Suri, R. and Kapoor, A. (2015) Will Social Media kill branding, Business Horizons, Vol. 58, pp. 35-44

Kolowich, L. (2017) 10 of the Best Brands on Twitter, https://blog.hub-spot.com/marketing/twitter-best-brands, accessed 11th February 2017

Kolowich, L. (2017) 10 of the Best Brands on Snapchat right now, https://blog.hubspot.com/marketing/snapchat-best-brands, accessed 14th February 2017

Komter, A. E. (2004) Gratitude and gift exchange, The Psychology of Gratitude, Robert A. Emmons and Michael E. McCullough, eds., pp. 195-213

Korporaal, G. (2015) 'The Changing Face of Cosmetics', The Deal, 20th March, pp. 28-21

Kotler, P. (1972) A Generic Concept of Marketing, Journal of Marketing, Vol. 36 April, pp. 46-54

Kotler, P. (1992) Marketing's new paradigm: what's really happening out there?, Planning Review, 20 (5), pp. 50-52

Kotler, P. (1994) Marketing Management: Analysis, Planning, Implementation, and Control. Prentice-Hall, Inc., Englewood Cliffs, New Jersey

Kotler, P. (1997) Marketing Management: Analysis, planning, implementation and control (9th ed), Prentice Hall, Englewood Cliffs, NJ.

Kotler, P. (1997) Method for the millennium, Marketing Business, February, pp. 26-27

Kotler, P. (1999) Kotler on Marketing, Free Press, New York

Kotler, P. (2000) Marketing Management, 10th edition, Prentice Hall, Englewood Cliffs, NJ

Kotler, P., Armstrong, G. and Opresnik, M. O. (2016) Marketing: An Introduction, 13th ed., Pearson, New Jersey

Kotler, P., Keller, K. L. and Opresnik, M. O. (2017) Marketing Management, 15th ed., Pearson, Hallbergmoos

Kotter, J. P. and Schlesinger, L. A. (1979) Choosing strategies for change, Harvard Business Review, March-April, pp. 106-111

Kumar, N. (1999) 'Internet distribution strategies: Dilemmas for the incumbent', Mastering Information Management, Part 7, Electronic Commerce, Financial Times, 15 March

Kumar, N., Scheer, S. and Kotler, P. (2000) From Market Driven to Market Driving, European Management Journal, 18 (2), pp. 129-141

Kumar, V. and Shah, D. (2004) Pushing and Pulling on the Internet, Marketing Research, Spring2004, Vol. 16, Issue 1, pp. 28-33

Lambin, J. (1976) Advertising, Competition and Market Conduct in Oligopoly Over Time Amsterdam: North Holland-Elsevier

Lancaster, G. and Massingham, L. (2001) Marketing Management, 3rd ed., McGraw-Hill

Lane, W. R., King, K. W. and J. T. Russell (2005) Kleppner's advertising procedure, 16th ed., Prentice Hall, Upper Saddle River, New Jersey

Lannon, J. (1991) Developing brand strategies across borders, Marketing and Research Today, August, pp. 160-168

Lassar, W., Mittal, B. and Sharma, A. (1995) 'Measuring customer-based brand equity', Journal of Consumer Marketing, vol. 12, pp. 11-19

Lauterborn, R. (1990) New Marketing Litany: 4P's Passe: C-Words take over, Advertising Age, October 1, pp. 25-27

Lee, S.F., LO, K.K., Leung, R.F. and Ko, A.S.O. (2000) Strategy formulation framework for vocational education: integrating SWOT analysis, balanced scorecard, QFD methodology and MBNQA education criteria, Managerial Auditing Journal, 15/8, pp. 407-23

Lenskold, J. D. (2004) Customer-centric marketing ROI; Harvard Business Review, January/February, pp. 26-31

Lesly, P. (1998) The handbook of public relations and communications, McGraw-Hill, Maidenhead

Levitt, T. (1983) After the Sale is Over…, Harvard Business Review, 16, pp. 87-93

Levitt, T. (1986) The Marketing Imagination, New York, New York: Free Press

Linkon, N. (2004) Using e-mail marketing to build business, TACTICS, November, p. 16

Linton, I. (1995) Database marketing: Know what you customer wants, Pitman, London

Little, R. W. (1970) The Marketing Channel: Who Should Lead This Extra-corporate Organisation, *Journal of Marketing*, Vol. 34, January, pp. 31-38.

Luthans, F. (1997) Organisational behaviour, McGraw-Hill, New York

Maignan, I. and Ferrell, O. C. (2004) Corporate social responsibility and marketing: an integrated framework, Journal of the Academy of Marketing Science, 32(1), pp. 3-19

Mantague, J. (2019) 'Reframing the awareness funnel and lead nurturing strategies to increase B2B brand awareness and quality lead generation', Journal of Brand Strategy, 8(2), pp. 160-166

McGoldrick, P. J. and Davies, G. (1995) International Retailing: Trends and strategies, Pitman, London

McGorty, C. (2017) 4 Reasons Why Google Plus Marketing is Still Relevant, http://fatguymedia.com/4-reasons-why-google-plus-marketing-is-still-relevant/, accessed 14th February 2017

McKenna, R. (1991) Relationship Marketing: Successful Strategies for the Age of the Customer. Addison-Wesley Publishing Co., Reading, MA.

Meenaghan, T. (1996) 'Ambush marketing – a threat to corporate sponsorship', Sloan Management Review, Fall, pp. 103 – 13

Meyer, C. (2001) While Customers wait, add value, Harvard Business Review, Vol 79, No 7, pp. 24-25

Michaelidou, N. and Dibb, S. (2006) Using email questionnaires for research: Good practice in tackling non-response, Journal of Targeting, Measurement and Analysis for Marketing, 14(4): 289–96.

Middleton, T. (2002) Sending out the winning message, Marketing Week, 16 May, pp. 43-45

Mills, J. F. and Camek, V. (2004) The risks, threats and opportunities of disintermediation: A distributor's view, International Journal of Physical Distribution and Logistics Management, 34(9), pp. 714-727

Mintz, O. and Currim, I. S. (2013) What drives Managerial Use of Marketing and Financial Metrics and Does Metric Use Affect Performance of Marketing-Mix Activities. Journal of Marketing, 77(March): 17-40

Morgan, R. M. (2000) Relationship marketing and marketing, in Shet, J. N. and Parvakiyar, A. (eds) Handbook of Relationship Marketing, Thousand Oaks, pp. 481-504

Morgan, R. M. and Hunt, S. D. (1994) The commitment-trust theory of relationship marketing, Journal of Marketing, 58 (3), pp. 20-38

Mort, G.S. and Drennan, J. (2002), Mobile digital technology: Emerging issues for Marketing, Journal of Database Marketing & Customer Strategy Management, Vol. 10, 1, September, pp. 9-23

Mueller, B. (1996) International Advertising: Communicating across cultures, Wadsworth, Belmont, CA

Mullane, J. V. (2002) The mission statement is a strategic tool: when used properly, Management Decision, Vol. 40, No. 5, pp. 448-455

Murphy, D. (2001) Dare to be digital, Marketing Business, December/January, pp. 3-5

Nagle, T. and Holden, R. (2001) The strategy and the tactics of pricing, 3rd ed., Prentice-Hall, Englewood Cliffs, New Jersey

Narver, J. C. and Slater, S. F. (1990) The effect of market orientation on business profitability, Journal of Marketing, 54, pp. 20-35.

Nørmark, P. (1994) 'Co-promotion in growth', Markedsføring (Danish marketing magazine), no. 14, p. 14

O'brian, S. and Ford, R. (1988) Can we at last say goodbye to social class?, Journal of the Market Research Society, 30(3), pp. 289-332

Omar, B., & Dequan, W. (2020). Watch, Share or Create: The Influence of Personality Traits and User Motivation on TikTok Mobile Video Usage. International Journal of Interactive Mobile Technologies (iJIM), 14(04), 121-137

Ottesen, O. (1995) 'Buyer initiative: ignored, but imperative for marketing management – towards a new view of market communication', Tidsvise Skrifter, no. 15, avdeling for Åkonomi, Kultur og Samfunnsfag ved Høgskolen i Stavanger

Owen, J. (2009) How to manage: the art of making things happen, 2nd ed., Pearson Prentice-Hall, Harlow

Palmatier, R. W., Dant, R. P., Grewal, D. and Evans, K. R. (2006) Factors influencing the effectiveness of relationship marketing: a meta-analysis, Journal of Marketing, 70 (October), pp. 136-153

Palmatier, R. W., Jarvis, C. B., Bechkoff, J. R. and Kardes, F. R. (2009) The Role Of Customer Gratitude In Relationship Marketing, Journal of Marketing, Vol 73 (September 2009), pp. 1-18

Patterson, B. (2016) 5 Yelp Facts Business Owners Should Know (But Most Don't), http://marketingland.com/5-yelp-facts-business-owners-should-know-163054, accessed 27th February 2017

Paul, P. (1996) 'Marketing on the Internet', Journal of Consumer Marketing, vol. 13, no. 4, pp. 27-39

Payne, A., Christopher, M. and Peck, H. (eds) (1995) Relationship Marketing for Competitive Advantage: Winning and Keeping Customers, Oxford, Butterworth Heinemann

Peattie, K. and Peattie, S. (1993) Sales Promotion: Playing to win?, Journal of Marketing Management, 9, pp. 255-269

Pels, J. (1999) Exchange relationships in consumer markets?, European Journal of Marketing, 33 (1/2), pp. 19-37

Pitt, L. F., Ewing, M. T. and Berthon, P. (2000) Turning Competitive Advantages into Customer Equity, Business Horizons, September-October, pp. 11-18.

Pitta, D. A. (1998), marketing one-to-one and its dependence on knowledge discovery in databases, Journal of Consumer Marketing, Vol. 15 No. 5, pp. 468-480

Porter, M. (1980), Competitive strategy, Free Press, New York, NY

Porter, M. E. (1985) Competitive Advantage, The Free Press, New York.

Prahalad, C. K. and Hamel, G. (1990) The Core Competence of the Corporation, Harvard Business Review, May-June, pp. 79-91

Pressey, A. D. and Mathews, B. P. (1998) Relationship marketing and retailing: comfortable bedfellows?, Customer Relationship Management, 1 (1), pp. 39-53

Ratten, V. (2015) 'International Consumer Attitudes Toward Cloud Computing: A Social Cognitive Theory and Technology Acceptance Model Perspective', Thunderbird International Business Review, Vol. 57, No. 3, May/June, pp. 217-228.

Reichheld, F. F. (1996) The Loyalty Effect: The Hidden Force Behind Growth, Profits and Lasting Value, Boston, Harvard Business School Press

Reichheld, F. F. (2003) The one number you need, Harvard Business Review, December, pp. 46-54

Ries, A. and Trout, J. (1981) Positioning: The battle for your mind, McGraw-Hill, New York

Robbins, S. P and Coulter, M. (2005) Management, 8th ed., Prentice Hall, New Jersey

Rogers, R. M. (2003) Diffusion of innovations, Free Press, New York

Rosenberg, L. J. and Cziepiel, J. A. (1984) A Marketing Approach to Customer Retention, Journal of Consumer Marketing, Vol. 1, Spring, pp.45-51.

Rothschild, M. L. (1978) Advertising strategies for high and low involvement situations, American Marketing Association Educator's Proceedings, Chicago, pp. 150-162

Rothschild, M. L. and Gaidis, W. C. (1981) Behavioural Learning Theory: Its relevance to marketing and promotions, Journal of Marketing, 45, Spring, pp. 70-78

Rust, R. T. and Zahorik, A. J. (1993) Customer Satisfaction, Customer Retention, and Market Share, Journal of Retailing, 69 (Summer), pp. 193-215.

Rust, R. T., Moorman, C. and Bhalla, G. (2010) Rethinking Marketing, Harvard Business Review, January-February 2010, pp. 94-101

Rust, R., Lemon, K. and Zeithaml, V. (2004) Return on Marketing: Using customer equity to focus marketing strategy, Journal of Marketing, January, p. 109

Rust, T. M., Ambler, T., Carpenter, G. C., Kumar, V. and Srivastava, R. K. (2004) 'Measuring Marketing Productivity: Current knowledge and Future directions', Journal of Marketing Vol. 68, October, pp. 76–89

Sampson, P. (1992) People are people the world over: The case for psychological market segmentation, European Journal of Marketing, 28(10), pp. 236-244

Sanyal, R.N. and Samanta, S.K. (2004), 'Determinants of Bribery in International Business', Thunderbird International Business Review, Vol. 46, March-April, pp. 133-148

Saunders, J. (2016) 'Should companies be creators on YouTube?', Market Leader, Quarter 2, pp. 36-39

Schögel, M. and Mrkwicka, K. (2011) 'Communication shift, Chancen und Herausforderungen aus Marketingsicht, Marketing Review St. Gallen, No. 5, pp. 6-10

Sciarrino, J., Friedman, J., Kirk, T., Kitchings, K.S. and Prudente, J. (2018) 'Quantifying the importance, contribution and efficiency of Cotton Inc.'s paid owned and earned media through customer journey modelling', Journal of Digital & Social Media Marketing, 6(4), pp. 294-311

Scott D. M. (2015) The New Rules of Marketing & PR, 5th ed., John Wiley & Sons, Inc, New York

Shapiro, B. P. and Wyman, J. (1981) New Ways to Reach Your Customer, Harvard Business Review, (July-August), pp. 103-110

Shelly, B. (1995) 'Cool customer', Unilever Magazine, no. 2, pp. 13-17

Sheth, J. N. and Parvatiyar, A. (1995) The evolution of relationship marketing, International Business Review, 4 (4), pp. 397-418

Sheth, J. N. and Sisodia, R. S. (1999) Revisiting marketing's law like generalizations, Journal of the Academy of Marketing Sciences, 17 (1), pp. 71-87

Sheth, J. N., Gardner, D. M. and Garett, D. E. (1988) Marketing Theory: Evolution and Evaluation. John Wiley & Sons, Inc, New York

Siu, E. (2016) 10 Ways to Use Snapchat for Business, http://www.socialmediaexaminer.com/10-ways-to-use-snapchat-for-business/, accessed 14th February 2017

Sloane, G. (2014) General Electric's First Snapchat Is One Small Step for Brand Kind, http://www.adweek.com/digital/general-electrics-first-snapchat-one-small-step-brand-kind-158921/, accessed 14th February 2017

Shrivastava, P. and Souder, W. E. (1987) The strategic management of technical innovation: A review and a model, Journal of Management Studies, 24(1), pp. 24-41

Silverman, G. (2005) Is 'it' the future of advertising?, Financial Times, 24 January, p. 11

Simms, J. (2001) The value of disclosure, Marketing, 2 August, pp. 26-27

Simon, C. J. and Sullivan, M. W. (1990) 'The measurement and determinants of brand equity: a financial approach', working paper, Graduate School of Business, University of Chicago, Chicago, Ill

Singleton, D. and Zyman, S. (2004) Segmenting opportunity, Brand Strategy, June, pp. 52-53

Singca, R. (2016) Tumblr Marketing Tips for Your Business, http://blog.swat.io/2016/12/13/tumblr-marketing-tips-for-your-business/, accessed 14th February 2017

Siu, E. (2016) 4 Tips to Improve Your YouTube Marketing, http://www.socialmediaexaminer.com/4-tips-to-improve-your-youtube-marketing/, accessed 7th March 2017

Slater, S. F. and Narver, J. C. (1996) Competitive strategy in the market-focused business, Journal of Market-Focused Management, Vol. 1, pp. 159-74

Smith, P. R. and Taylor, J. (2004) Marketing Communications: An integrated approach, Kogan Page, London

Smith, M. (2010) 'Facebook 101 for Business: Your Complete Guide.' Social Media Examiner (August 10). http://www.socialmediaexaminer.com/facebook-101-business-guide/, accessed 25th January 2017

Stone, M. (2002) Multichannel customer management: The benefits and challenges, Journal of Database Marketing, Vol. 10, pp. 39-52

Stone, M., Davis, D. and Bond, A. (1995) Direct hit: Direct Marketing with a winning edge, Pitman, London

Storbacka, K., Strandvik, T. and Grönroos, C. (1994) Managing customer relations for profit: the dynamics of relationship quality, International Journal of Service Industry, Management, 5, pp. 21-38

Straker, K. and Wrigley, C. (2016), Emotionally engaging customers in the digital age: the case study of 'Burberry Love', Journal of Fashion Marketing and Management, Vol. 20, No. 3, 276-299

Strebel, P. (1996) Why do employees resist change?, Harvard Business Review, May-June, pp. 86-92

Stroud, D. (2008) Social networking: an age-neutral commodity – Social networking becomes a mature web application, Journal of Direct, Data and Digital Marketing Practice, Vol. 9, No. 3, pp. 278-292

Swaminathan, V., Fox, R. J. and Reddy, S. K. (2001) The impact of brand extension introduction on choice, Journal of Marketing, October, pp. 1-15

Szigin, I., Canning, L., Rappel, A. (2005) Online community: enhancing the relationship marketing concept through customer bonding, International Journal of Service Industry Management, Vol. 16, No. 5, pp. 480-496

Solon, O. (2017) Facebook Watch takes on YouTube and TV with re-vamped video offering, The Guardian (August 10), https://www.theguardian.com/technology/2017/aug/09/facebook-new-video-feature-watch-youtube-rival, accessed 10th August 2017

Thomke, S. (2019) 'The Magic That Makes Customer Experiences Stick', MIT Sloan Management Review, Fall Issue, 61(1), pp. 56-63

Toyne, B. and Walters, P. G. P. (1993) Global Marketing Management: A strategic perspective (2nd ed), Allyn and Bacon, Needham Heights, MA

Treacy, M. and Wiersema, F. (1993) Customer intimacy and other Value Disciplines, Harvard Business Review, January-February, pp. 84-93

Tuten, T.L. and Solomon, M.R. (2015), Social Media Marketing, 2nd ed., Sage Publications Ltd.

Tuten, T.L. (2020) Principles of Marketing – for the Digital Age, 1st ed., Sage Publications Ltd, London

Valentine, M. (2009) It's all in the mind, Marketing Week, 2 April, p. 29

Varadarajan, P. R. and Cunningham, M. H. (2000) Strategic alliances: a synthesis of conceptual foundations, in Shet, J. N. and Parvatiyar, A. (Eds) Handbook of Relationship Marketing, Thousand Oaks, CA: Sage, pp. 271-302

Visser, M., Sikkenga, B. and Berry, M. (2018) Digital Marketing Fundamentals – From Strategy to ROI, 1st ed., Noordhoff Uitgevers, Groningen/Utrecht

Webb, T. (2008) Apple's Guru Calls a New Tune, Observer, 15 June, p. 6

Webster, F. E. and Wind, Y. (1972) Organisational Buying Behaviour, Prentice-Hall, New Jersey

Webster, F. E., Jr. (1992) The Changing Role of Marketing in the Corporation, Journal of Marketing, Vol. 56, No. 4 (October), pp. 1-17

Young, Steve P. (2013) The 2013 YouTube Marketing Guide, https://blog.kissmetrics.com/2013-youtube-marketing-guide/, accessed 7th March 2017

Zarella, D. (2010) The social media marketing book, O'Reilly, California

About the authors

Svend Hollensen (svend@sam.sdu.dk) is an Associate Professor of International Marketing at University of Southern Denmark (Sønderborg) and a visiting professor at London Metropolitan University and University of Naples Federico II.

He is the author of globally published textbooks, including the best seller 'Global Marketing', 7th Edition (Pearson) which was published in 2017 and is no. 1 in sales outside United States, and no. 2 worldwide (in the segment 'International Marketing' textbooks). Indian and Spanish editions have been developed in co-operation with co-authors. The textbook Global Marketing has also been translated into Chinese, Russian, Spanish and Dutch.

His 'Marketing Management – A Relationship Approach', 3rd edition (Pearson) was published in 2015. He has been publishing articles in well-recognized journals like California Management Review, Journal of Business Strategy, Journal of Family Business Strategy and Marketing Intelligence & Planning.

Through his company, Hollensen ApS (CVR 25548299), Svend has also worked as a business consultant for several multinational companies, as well as global organizations like the World Bank.

Philip Kotler is S. C. Johnson & Son Distinguished Professor of International Marketing at the Kellogg School of Management, Northwestern University. He received his master s degree at the University of Chicago and his Ph.D. at M.I.T., both in economics. Dr. Kotler is author of 'Marketing Management' (Pearson), now in its fifteenth edition and the most widely used marketing text book in graduate schools of business worldwide. He has authored dozens of other successful books and has written more than 100 articles in leading journals. He is the only three-time winner of the coveted Alpha Kappa Psi award for the best annual article in the 'Journal of Marketing.' Professor Kotler was named the first recipient of four major awards: the 'Distinguished Marketing Educator of the Year Award' and the 'William L. Wilkie Marketing for a Better World Award,' both given by the American Marketing Association; the 'Philip Kotler Award for Excellence in Health Care Marketing' presented by the Academy for Health Care Services Marketing; and the 'Sheth Foundation Medal for Exceptional Contribution to Marketing Scholarship and Practice.' His numerous other major honors include the Sales and Marketing Executives International' Marketing Educator of the Year Award; 'The European Association of Marketing Consultants and Trainers 'Marketing Excellence Award', the 'Charles Coolidge Parlin Marketing Research Award' and the 'Paul D. Converse Award', given by the American Marketing Association to honor outstanding contributions to science in marketing. A recent Forbes survey ranks Professor Kotler in the top 10 of the world's most influential business thinkers. And in a recent 'Financial Times' poll of 1,000 senior executives across the world, Professor Kotler was ranked as the fourth most influential business writer/guru of the twenty-first century. Dr. Kotler has served as chairman of the College on Marketing of the Institute of Management Sciences, a director of the American Marketing Association, and a trustee of the Marketing Science Institute. He has consulted with many major U.S. and international companies in the areas of marketing strategy and planning, marketing organization, and international marketing. He has traveled and lectured extensively throughout Europe, Asia, and South America, advising companies and governments about global marketing practices and opportunities.

Marc Oliver Opresnik (Marc@kotlerimpact.org ; http://bit.ly/Opresnik-Management-Consulting) is a Professor of Marketing and Management and Member of the Board of Directors at SGMI St. Gallen Management Institute, a leading international business school. In addition, he is a Professor of Business Administration at the Technische Hochschule Lübeck as well as a visiting professor to international universities such as Regent's University London and East China University of Science and Technology in Shanghai. He has 10 years of experience working in senior management and marketing positions for Shell International Petroleum Co. Ltd.

Dr. Opresnik is the author of numerous articles and books. Along with Kevin Keller and Phil Kotler, he is co-author of the German edition of "Marketing Management", the "Bible of Marketing". Dr. Opresnik also was chosen to be the co-author with Phil Kotler and Gary Armstrong of the Global Edition of "Marketing: An Introduction", which is one of the world's most widely used marketing text books. In addition, he is co-editor and member of the editorial board of several international journals such as "Transnational Marketing", „Journal of World Marketing Summit Group" and „International Journal of New Technologies in Science and Engineering".

With effect from March 2014, he was appointed "Chief Research Officer" at "Kotler Impact Inc.", the internationally operating company of Phil Kotler. In addition, he was appointed "Chief Executive Officer" of the Kotler Business Programme, an initiative to enhance marketing education worldwide via online and offline learning with Pearson as global educational partner.

As president of his consulting firm "Opresnik Management Consulting" (https://www.facebook.com/MarcOliverOpresnik ; www.opresnik-management-consulting.de) he works for numerous institutions, governments and international corporations including Google, Coca-Cola, McDonald's, SAP, Shell International Petroleum Co Ltd., Procter & Gamble, Unilever, L'Oréal, Bayer, BASF and adidas. More than 1/4 million people have benefited professionally and personally from his impulses and experienced him as a coach in seminars on marketing, sales and negotiation and as a speaker at conferences all over the world including locations such as St. Gallen, Berlin, Houston, Moscow, Kuala Lumpur, London, Paris, Dubai and Tokyo.

With his many years of international experience as a coach, keynote speaker and consultant, Marc Opresnik is one of the world's most renowned marketing, management and negotiation experts.

Index

Printed in Great Britain
by Amazon